BASEBALLOGY

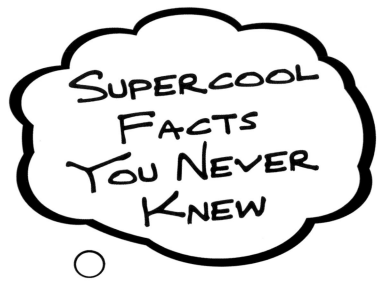

Supercool Facts You Never Knew

Written and Illustrated by
Kevin Sylvester

annick press
toronto + new york + vancouver

© 2015 Kevin Sylvester (art and text)
Edited by Linda Pruessen
Designed by Sheryl Shapiro

The charts and graphs in this book are meant for illustrative purposes only and do not necessarily reflect exact ratios or measurements.

Thanks to Baseball Almanac for the stats on birthplace (pp 22—23). Researcher Mark Armour did amazing work on the ethnicity of ball players. You can check out his study at sabr.org/bioproj/topic/baseball-demographics —1947—2012. And thanks to baseball-reference.com for data on birthplaces from the beginning of the game to today (pp 22—25), and for being an amazing source of box scores, player profiles, and baseball records.

We acknowledge the support of the Canada Council for the Arts, the Ontario Arts Council, and the Government of Canada through the Canada Book Fund (CBF) for our publishing activities.

Cataloging in Publication

Sylvester, Kevin, author, illustrator
        Baseballogy : supercool facts you never knew / written and illustrated by Kevin Sylvester.

Includes bibliographical references and index.
Issued in print and electronic formats.
ISBN 978-1-55451-708-4 (bound).—978-1-55451-707-7 (pbk.).—
ISBN 978-1-55451-710-7 (pdf).—ISBN 978-1-55451-709-1 (html)

        1. Baseball—Miscellanea—Juvenile literature. I. Title.

GV867.5.S94 2015   j796.357   C2014-905900-0
                                               C2014-905901-9

Distributed in Canada by:
Firefly Books Ltd.
50 Staples Avenue, Unit 1
Richmond Hill, ON L4B 0A7
Published in the U.S.A. by Annick Press (U.S.) Ltd.

Distributed in the U.S.A. by:
Firefly Books (U.S.) Inc.
P.O. Box 1338
Ellicott Station
Buffalo, NY 14205

Printed in China

Visit us at: www.annickpress.com
Visit Kevin Sylvester at: kevinsylvesterbooks.com

Also available in e-book format. Please visit www.annickpress.com/ebooks.html for more details. Or scan

This book is dedicated to so many baseball lovers in my life:
John Sliwa, who gave me a signed Ron Santo baseball
Vince Carlin, who misses his Brooklyn Dodgers
My brother Doug, co-owner of team Norwides!
And my Mum (a catcher) and Dad (a pitcher)!

CONTENTS

INTRODUCTION

Baseball seems sooooo simple when you are watching from the stands.

The pitcher throws the ball.

The batter tries to hit it.

And when that ball does get hit, the fielders try to catch it and get the batter out.

But there's so much more to baseball than throwing, hitting, running, and catching. A lot of what makes baseball such an amazing game is hidden, visible only to those in the know. This book is going to put you in the know. It's going to rip the cover off that baseball (literally, on page 6!) and show you all the stuff that's hidden under the surface.

Did you know, for example, that each and every pitch is a complex web of possibilities? The pitcher is trying to mess with the batter's brain and muscles. The batter has spent more time researching that pitcher than you have on your homework. And the difference between a hit and a swinging strike? Math.

Over the last few decades, there's been a math and numbers explosion in baseball. Thirty years ago, a .300 hitter (a player who gets a hit 3 out of every 10 times at bat) was a superstar. Today, many teams are happier with a .250 hitter (who gets a hit about a quarter of the time) who also gets walks and can field.

Why? You'll find out inside.

Do you play baseball? What do you think your chances are of making the big leagues? We'll look into that.

We'll explore whether a player from a hundred years ago could suit up and fit in to one of today's games, and what a fan from the past might think about a current-day outing to the ballpark.

And we'll answer some pretty weird questions:

What animal part was once used as the center of a baseball?

How many hot dogs did the great Babe Ruth eat before he had to be rushed to the hospital?

After reading this book, you'll never see baseball in the same way again.

Prepare to have your mind blown.

ALL ABOUT THE BALL

A baseball is like a little universe. It seems so small, so compact. But take a look at what's inside, and it goes on and on. How does all that stuff fit in one little package?

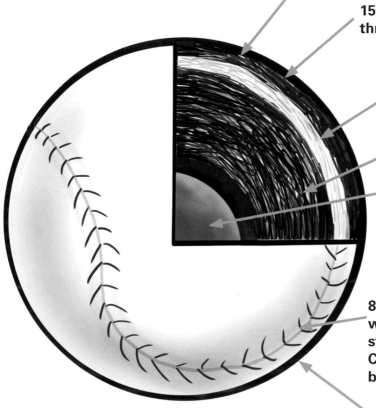

450 feet (137 meters) of fine poly/cotton yarn. This is covered in adhesive to hold the inside together.

159 feet (48.5 meters) of three-ply gray yarn.

135 feet (41 meters) of three-ply white yarn.

363 feet (110.5 meters) of four-ply gray yarn.

The "pill" —a cork center surrounded by two rubber layers. The pill weighs seven eighths of an ounce (25 grams) with a circumference of roughly 4.5 inches (11.5 centimeters).

88 inches (223.52 centimeters) of waxed red thread is used. That's 108 stitches, hand-stitched by workers in Costa Rica at the rate of about three baseballs per hour.

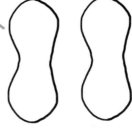

2 figure-8 sections of white cowhide. The leather needs to be white and smooth. Number one grade, alum-tanned full-grained cowhide, primarily from Midwest Holstein cattle, dyed white, is preferred. Before each game, the ball is rubbed down with a particular mud (Lena Blackburne Baseball Rubbing Mud from some secret location near the Delaware River) to make it less shiny and less slick.

The baseball has a circumference of between 9 and 9.25 inches (22.86–23.5 centimeters). It weighs between 5 and 5.25 ounces (141.5–156 grams).

More than a million baseballs a year are ordered by major league baseball (MLB). These are used for games—at a rate of about a hundred or so per game—and also for batting practice, giveaways, souvenirs, and so on.

The center of a baseball needs to be a little spongy. It helps the ball bounce off the bat. In the beginning, rubber wasn't widely available. So people used whatever was available. It could be cork, or (in some cases) fish eyes. Yes, baseball makers used actual fish eyes—spongy and round!

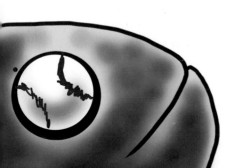

1 baseball = about 1,107 feet (337 meters) of yarn. Unraveled, that would just about reach the roof of the Empire State Building.

GLOVES

Fielders use different gloves for different positions, and there are specific rules about how big the gloves can be.

Outfielders use the longest gloves possible, to help them make those amazing "fingertip" catches.

Infielders tend to use smaller gloves, to more easily get the ball out of the webbing and into their throwing hand.

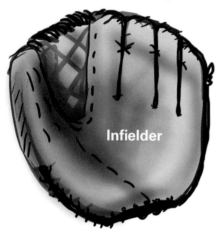

Infielder

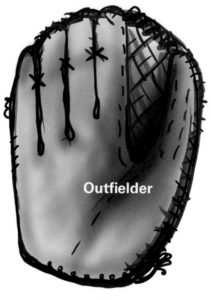

Outfielder

Catcher's

First baseman

First basemen and catchers receive a lot of hard throws, so they are allowed bigger gloves with more padding.

When baseball was young, players didn't wear gloves. But after years of bruises and broken fingers, a few started using normal work gloves. The padding got thicker and thicker over the years until players ended up with the large leather gloves they wear today.

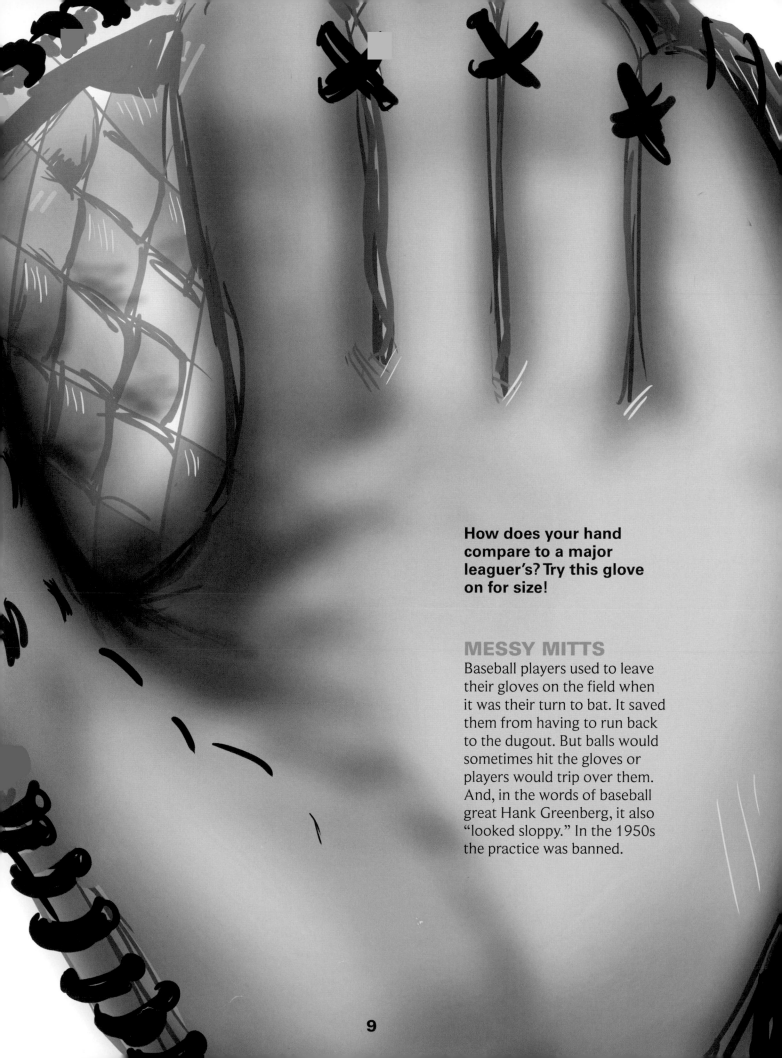

How does your hand compare to a major leaguer's? Try this glove on for size!

MESSY MITTS

Baseball players used to leave their gloves on the field when it was their turn to bat. It saved them from having to run back to the dugout. But balls would sometimes hit the gloves or players would trip over them. And, in the words of baseball great Hank Greenberg, it also "looked sloppy." In the 1950s the practice was banned.

BATS AND HELMETS

Players are very particular about their bats. Some even give them names. Shoeless Joe Jackson called his Black Betsy. Babe Ruth called his War Club.

One thing all bats have in common? In the major leagues, they are all made of wood. They used to be all made from ash trees, but bat makers are now using other woods too. One reason for the emergence of the new wooden bats is a bug—the emerald ash borer. This pest came over from Asia and has been eating its way through North America's ash trees.

Why wood? Baseball is a sport that embraces traditions. The crack of the bat is one of the constants. The ping of an aluminum bat or composite bat (made with aluminum and other materials) might be fine for lower leagues and kids' leagues, but not for the pros.

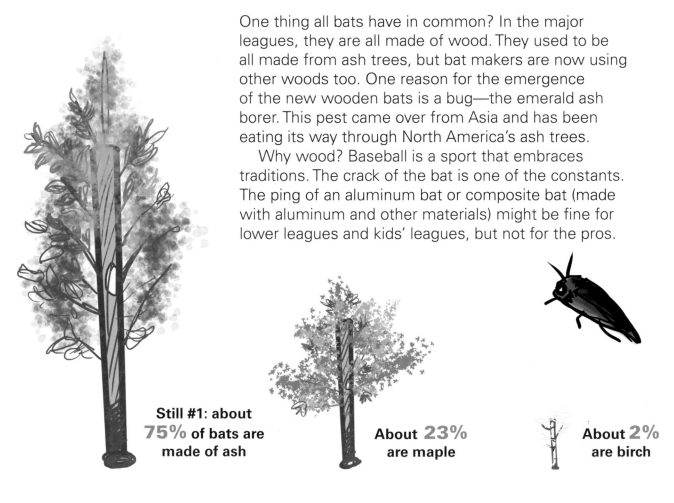

Still #1: about 75% of bats are made of ash

About 23% are maple

About 2% are birch

A bat gets broken about every other major league baseball game.

**Fungo bat
15–20 ounces
(425-567 grams)**

**Normal bat
30+ ounces
(850.5+ grams)**

Coaches use a "fungo bat" to help warm up the fielders before games. It's thinner and weighs less than a normal bat so coaches can hit lots of balls to the fielders without getting tired. As for its name, that remains one of the game's great mysteries.

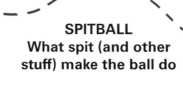

FASTBALL
What a normal pitch does in the air

SPITBALL
What spit (and other stuff) make the ball do

1917

1947

1967

Today

THE EVOLUTION OF THE BATTING HELMET

You'd think batting helmets would be as old as gloves in baseball history.

Not even close. Which is weird.

In 1920, Ray Chapman was killed when a spitball pitch hit his head. His death led to a very fast rule change. Umpires were ordered to replace balls that became dirty and too hard to see, and they soon banned spitballs altogether.

But it took another 30 years before most players starting protecting their brains. Bob Montgomery was the last player to bat without a helmet. He retired in 1979.

Spit is not the only thing that can make the ball "dance": Vaseline, glue, shaving cream, and sunscreen also work. There are even stories of pitchers peeing in their pants to get a little something extra for the surface of the ball.

THE FIELD

While baseball has had many changes over the years, some things stay the same. The infield of every baseball diamond is a standard size. But outfields can change a lot.

In the old days, field dimensions could even change mid-game. Teams used to sell "on field" tickets for play offs, setting up temporary seats right on the field. Fans would move out of the way to help the home team, and not budge an inch for opposing players.

Toronto's field (below) is about as standard a field as they come.

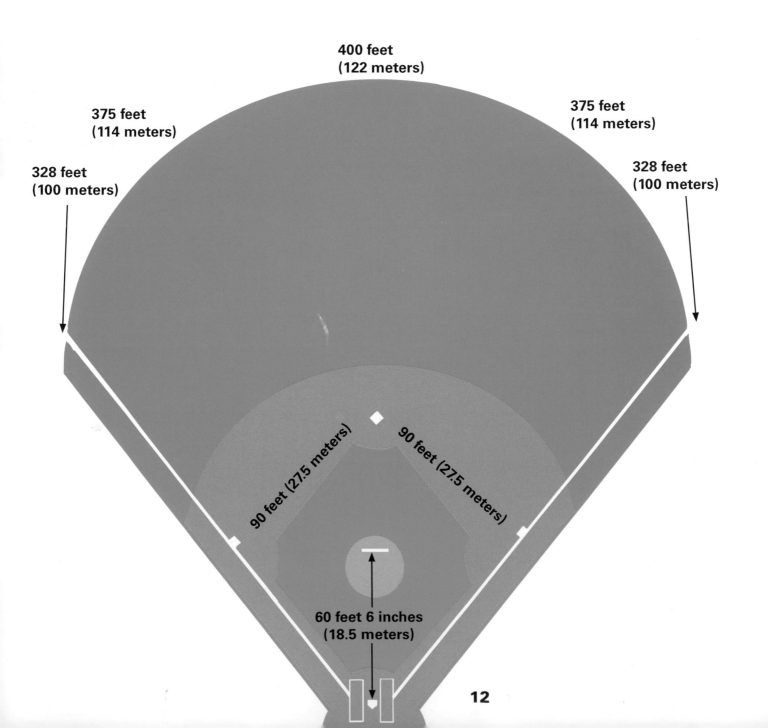

400 feet
(122 meters)

375 feet
(114 meters)

375 feet
(114 meters)

328 feet
(100 meters)

328 feet
(100 meters)

90 feet (27.5 meters)

90 feet (27.5 meters)

60 feet 6 inches
(18.5 meters)

Not all ballparks are standard.
The yellow line below shows the closest outfield walls in the major leagues.
The red line shows how far away those can get in some parks.

Fenway Park in Boston is perhaps the strangest field of all. The "Green Monster" is a giant outfield wall. It's 37 feet, 2 inches tall (11.5 meters). Batters can bounce the ball off the wall for a hit, and the left fielder has to be ready to play all the wacky angles.

And imagine how far away center field feels if you are standing at the plate in Houston. That's a long way to hit a ball.

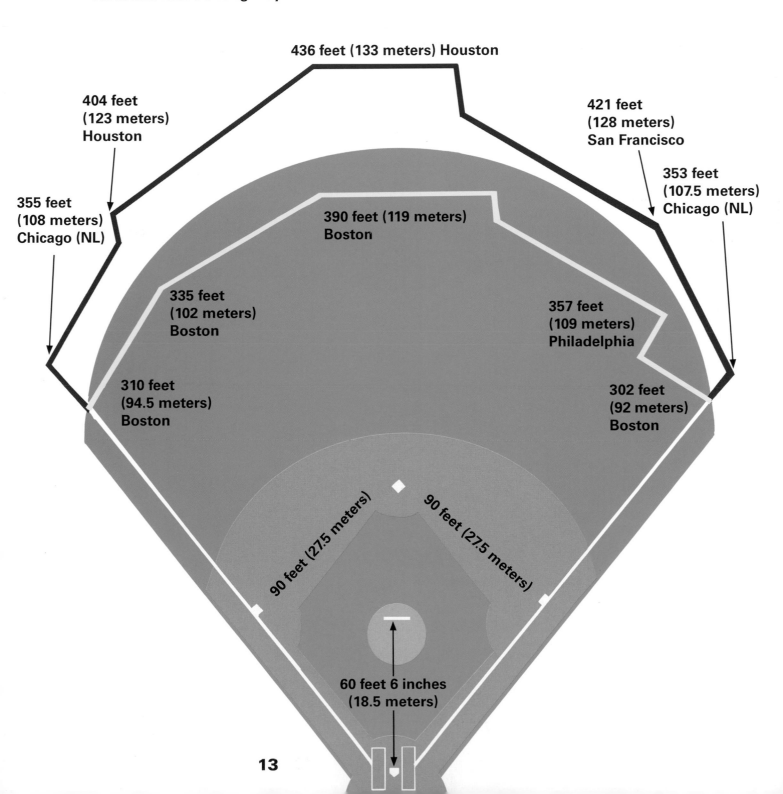

436 feet (133 meters) Houston

404 feet
(123 meters)
Houston

421 feet
(128 meters)
San Francisco

355 feet
(108 meters)
Chicago (NL)

390 feet (119 meters)
Boston

353 feet
(107.5 meters)
Chicago (NL)

335 feet
(102 meters)
Boston

357 feet
(109 meters)
Philadelphia

310 feet
(94.5 meters)
Boston

302 feet
(92 meters)
Boston

90 feet (27.5 meters)

90 feet (27.5 meters)

60 feet 6 inches
(18.5 meters)

THE STADIUM, THE FANS!

Fans make the game fun. They do the cheering, eat the food, drink the drinks (and also pay most of the bills).

115,000
BIGGEST CROWD EVER!
The L.A. Dodgers played a game in a football stadium in 2008.

(Runner up: Australia hosted an exhibition game at the Melbourne Cricket Grounds in 1956 that drew **114,000 fans**.)

The Colorado Rockies hold the record for most fans over a whole season—
4,483,350
in 1993.

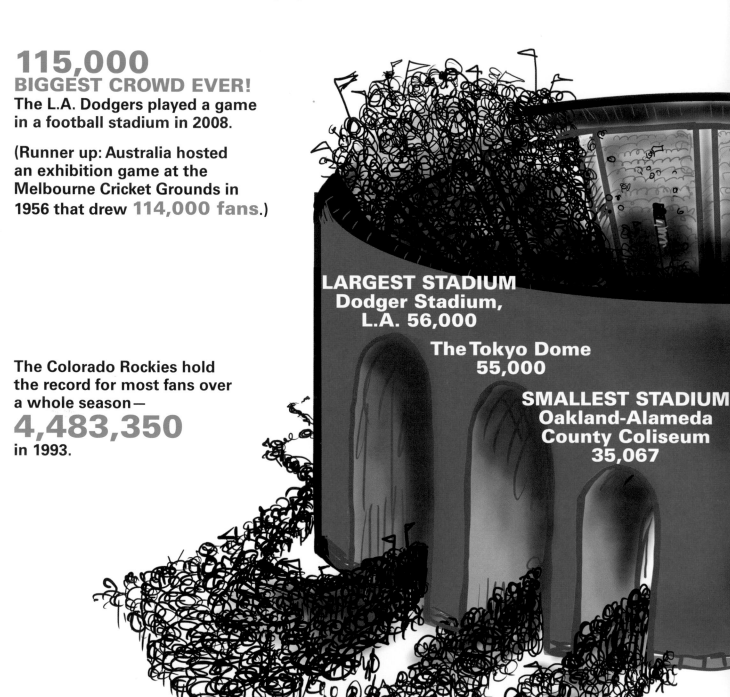

LARGEST STADIUM
Dodger Stadium,
L.A. 56,000

The Tokyo Dome
55,000

SMALLEST STADIUM
Oakland-Alameda
County Coliseum
35,067

653
SMALLEST CROWD EVER!
April 1979, Oakland beat Seattle 6-5

(Honorable mention: Miami sold 10,000 tickets for a game in 2011. Only 347 showed up— but Hurricane Irene was blowing through Florida at the time, so that's understandable.)

Baseball parks are giant networks of concrete and steel. And they are expensive!

Old Yankee Stadium was state of the art in 1923. It cost $2.5 million to build. That would equal about $35 million in today's dollars.

But when the Yankees built their new ballpark—opened in 2012 in the Bronx, New York—they decided to go for the best of everything: more than 50 private boxes, a massive video screen, stone walkways, dozens of concession stands, and mini-museums tucked into the main hallways. It cost closer to $1.5 billion (or $107 million in 1923 dollars).

Who pays for that? You do. Cities chip in tax incentives and sometimes direct money to cover some of the costs, and the teams pay a lot. But they get that money back from you in the form of fees for watching on TV and, of course, ticket sales.

NIGHT LIGHT

Until the 1930s, baseball games were almost all played during the day. Kansas City of the Negro Leagues started playing under lights in 1930. The first major league night game was in Cincinnati in 1935. Now there are only a handful of games played before 7 p.m., and most of those are on weekends.

TAKE ME OUT TO THE BALL GAME

Your grandma had a different experience at the ballpark than you do. Sure, the game was pretty much the same, but watching (and snacking!) was way cheaper.

1950

ice cream 10¢

popcorn 10¢

hot dog 30¢

soda 15¢

peanuts 10¢

pretzel 30¢

SECTION 24
SEAT 8A

CHICAGO

RESERVED SEAT
ENTER GATE C

$5

24
SEC.

SECTION 24
SEAT 8A

CHICAGO
VS.
NEW YORK

SEPTEMBER 3, 1950

RESERVED SEAT
ENTER GATE C

$5

24
SEC.

A
ROW

3
SEAT

Today

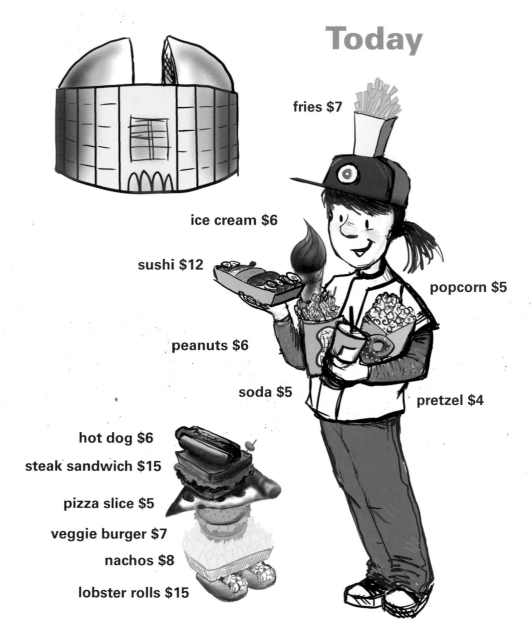

fries $7

ice cream $6

sushi $12

popcorn $5

peanuts $6

soda $5

pretzel $4

hot dog $6

steak sandwich $15

pizza slice $5

veggie burger $7

nachos $8

lobster rolls $15

Why are things more expensive today? Well, there's inflation. Making things is more expensive than it used to be, so the people who make cars, televisions, and the snacks you buy at the ballpark have to charge you more and more. Governments also print more physical money each year, which makes each individual bit of money worth less overall.

There are baseball reasons, too. New stadiums cost money. Players' salaries have gone up (a lot). Travel costs have increased too. A hundred years ago, most teams were a bus ride away from each other; now the major leagues are spread across the continent.

WACKY SNACKS

Some foods are a little out there. Colorado sells Rocky Mountain Oysters for $7.50. Those aren't really oysters. They are bull testicles.

Section 24
Seat 3A

New York
vs
Chicago

September 3, 2015

$50
Price

$50
Price

WHO GETS WHAT AND WHEN?

So how does the baseball economy work? Like any other businesses, owners bring money in from lots of sources, and send money out to lots of people.

Money In

ticket sales:	$100,000,000
national TV revenue:	$50,000,000
local TV revenue:	$50,000,000
stadium rentals (concerts, special events):	$10,000,000
digital/mobile content (apps and online purchases):	$3,000,000
advertising sales:	$10,000,000
naming rights:	$11,000,000
food sales:	$15,000,000
parking:	$10,000,000
Total:	**$259,000,000**

Baseball teams often sell the names to their fields. You've got Petco Park (San Diego), Rogers Centre (Toronto), U.S. Cellular Field (Chicago), and many more.

Money Out

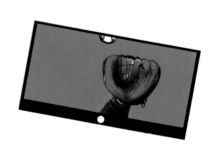

player salaries—for example, $3.2 million × 25 players:	$80,000,000
employee salaries, other office costs:	$25,000,000
costs to run the stadium:	$20,000,000
scouting:	$11,000,000
minor leagues (players, and infrastructure—ballparks, equipment):	$20,000,000
advertising:	$10,000,000
equipment:	$10,000,000
local taxes:	$2,000,000
broadcasting:	$3,000,000
long-term debt (for example, from buying the team):	$20,000,000
interest on loans and expenses:	$5,000,000
Total:	**$206,000,000**

Total in: **$259,000,000**
Total out: **–$206,000,000**
Net "profit":   **$53,000,000**

This is an average per team per season. Some teams (like the New York Yankees) can make way more money. Some can lose money. Also, this net "profit" has to cover federal taxes and other deductions, such as injury insurance for players, losses from non-baseball departments if the team is part of a large corporation, and so on. After all that, what's left might be split among dozens of co-owners or team shareholders.

BY THE NUMBERS

Time to play! Did you know that numbers can help you figure out a baseball game, even if you don't see the action yourself?

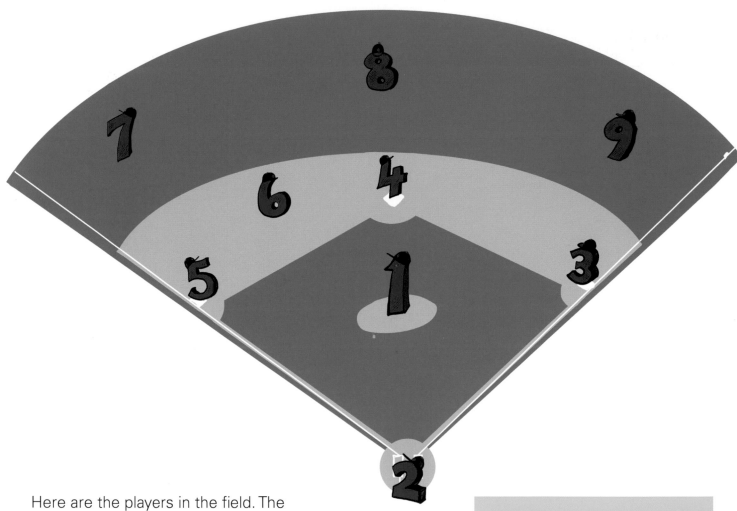

Here are the players in the field. The numbers represent their positions. The pitcher is 1. The catcher is 2. The first baseman is 3, and so on.

A radio announcer might say the batter hit into a "6-4-3 double play". That means the batter hit the ball to the shortstop (6), who threw to the second baseman (4), who touched second base for one out and then threw to first base (3) to get the batter out.

Or an announcer might say "E-7". That means the left fielder (7) made a mistake, an error. Maybe he dropped the ball, or made a bad throw.

Skill Test
See if you can use the number system to figure out what happened in these plays:
a) 1-3 out
b) E-9
c) 4-6-3 double play
d) 5-6 out
e) 7-2 out
f) 2-1 out

A player's number used to represent where they usually hit. Babe Ruth was #3 because he usually hit third in the lineup. Lou Gehrig was #4 because he was fourth. That's not the way numbers are used today.

Pitchers from Japan will often ask for #18 when they come to the major leagues. In Japan, #18 is reserved for the ace—the team's best pitcher.

In 1995, Omar Olivares wore #00 to represent his initials.

Who says #13 is unlucky? More than 200 players have worn it, including Dave Concepción from 1970 to 1988—19 years! Blue Moon Odom wore it for, appropriately, 13 seasons in the 1960s and 1970s. (He also had a great nickname.)

About a dozen players have worn #99.

Jackie Robinson wore #42. Why? It was just the number he was assigned when he became the first African-American player in the major leagues, in 1947. Baseball has since retired that number. On Jackie Robinson Day, everyone in the league wears #42.

Answers

a) the pitcher threw to first to record an out; b) the right fielder made an error; c) second baseman to shortstop to first for two outs; d) third baseman to shortstop (who was probably covering second base) for an out; e) the left fielder threw the ball to home for an out—probably an exciting play; f) catcher threw to pitcher (who was probably covering either the plate or first base) for an out.

21

THE CHANGING FACE OF THE MAJORS

When pro baseball started out, the players were almost exclusively from the United States. Boy, has that changed.

There were, of course, exceptions. Canadian Tip O'Neill played in the late 1900s and was one of the best hitters of all time.

Australian Joe Quinn pitched from 1884 to 1901.

And in the early days, the game was very popular with kids from immigrant families, many of whom were born in Germany, England, Ireland, and so on, but who lived in the United States.

THIS WAS THE MAKEUP OF THE GAME ABOUT 100 YEARS AGO.

32 of 791 players were not born in the United States. The non-U.S. players were from:

Canada: 7
Cuba: 7
Ireland: 5
Germany: 2
Sweden: 2
Atlantic Ocean*: 1
Austria-Hungary: 1
Denmark: 1
England: 1
France: 1
Russia: 1
Scotland: 1
Switzerland: 1
Wales: 1

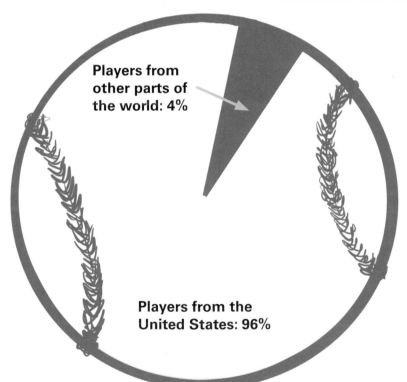

Players from other parts of the world: 4%

Players from the United States: 96%

*Yes, there was actually a player whose birthplace was listed as "Atlantic Ocean." In 1888, Ed Porray was born on a ship in international waters.

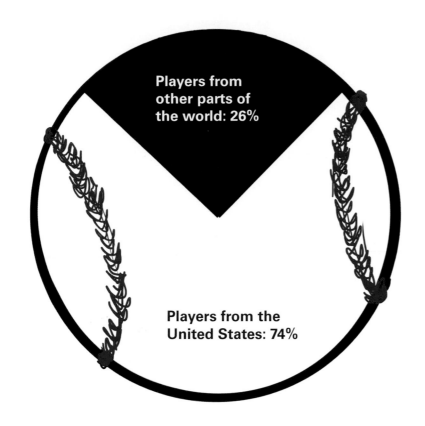

Players from other parts of the world: 26%

Players from the United States: 74%

This is the makeup from 2014.

270 of 1,027 players were not born in the United States. The non-U.S. players were from:
Dominican Republic: 103
Venezuela: 67
Cuba: 20
Canada: 15
Puerto Rico: 13
Mexico: 11
Japan: 10
Columbia: 4
Curacao: 4
Panama: 4
Australia: 3
Nicaragua: 3
Taiwan: 3
Brazil: 2
Germany: 2
South Korea: 2
Aruba: 1
Jamaica: 1
Netherlands: 1
Saudi Arabia: 1

Today, there are organized leagues on every continent, and almost all of them are sending players to the "bigs".

The World Baseball Classic—an international tournament—has been held three times. Japan has won twice and the Dominican Republic, once. The U.S. has not yet finished in the top three.

Opening Day games for the major leagues have been held in Japan, Mexico, Australia, and Puerto Rico.

Jackie Robinson broke the color barrier in 1947.

White
African-American
Latino
Asian

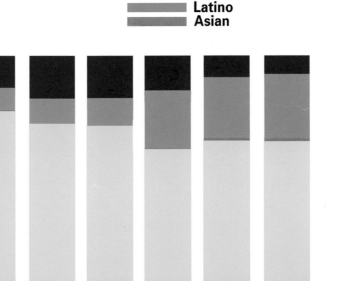

1947   1957   1967   1977   1987   1997   2007   TODAY

THE HISTORY OF THE GLOBAL GAME

Lots of things have helped grow baseball. Some stories suggest that American troops spread the sport globally as they traveled the world. Actually, economic trade, students, and teachers were the biggest factors.

Cuba formed a league in the late 1800s after it became an island retreat for rich Americans. It spread from there throughout Latin America.

Professor Horace Wilson was teaching in Japan when he introduced the sport there in the early 1870s. But it really caught on when Japanese student Hiroshi Hiraoka returned from a trip to the U.S. in 1878 with equipment and started a team.

DEBUTS FOR PLAYERS FROM DIFFERENT COUNTRIES

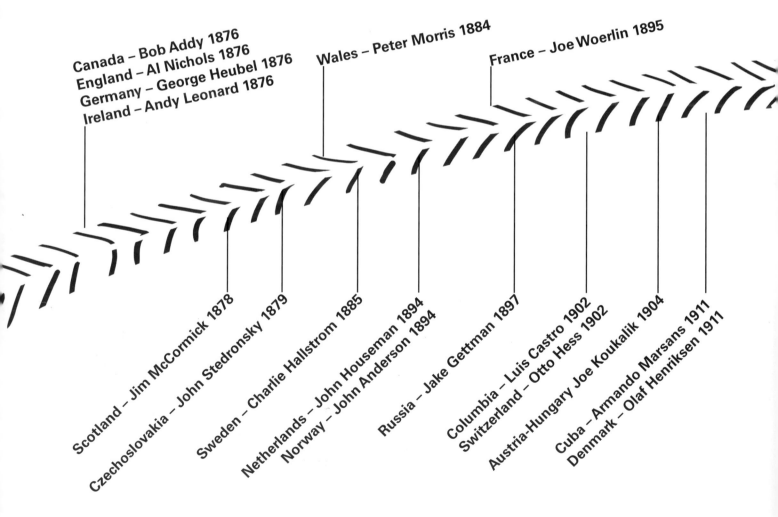

Canada – Bob Addy 1876
England – Al Nichols 1876
Germany – George Heubel 1876
Ireland – Andy Leonard 1876

Wales – Peter Morris 1884

France – Joe Woerlin 1895

Scotland – Jim McCormick 1878

Czechoslovakia – John Stedronsky 1879

Sweden – Charlie Hallstrom 1885

Netherlands – John Houseman 1894
Norway – John Anderson 1894

Russia – Jake Gettman 1897

Columbia – Luis Castro 1902
Switzerland – Otto Hess 1902

Austria-Hungary Joe Koukalik 1904

Cuba – Armando Marsans 1911
Denmark – Olaf Henriksen 1911

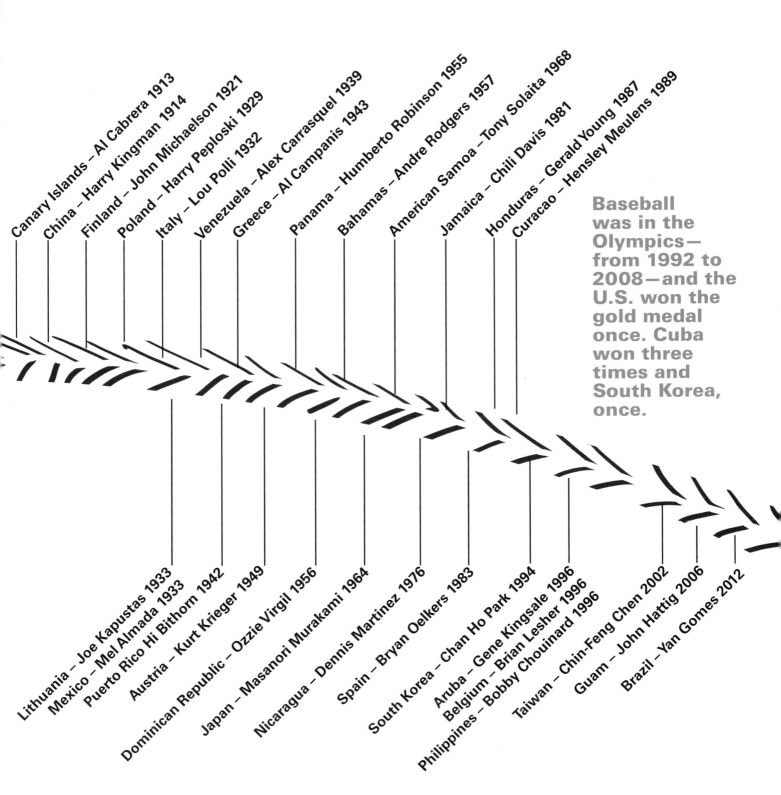

Canary Islands – Al Cabrera 1913
China – Harry Kingman 1914
Finland – John Michaelson 1921
Poland – Harry Peploski 1929
Italy – Lou Polli 1932
Venezuela – Alex Carrasquel 1939
Greece – Al Campanis 1943
Panama – Humberto Robinson 1955
Bahamas – Andre Rodgers 1957
American Samoa – Tony Solaita 1968
Jamaica – Chili Davis 1981
Honduras – Gerald Young 1987
Curacao – Hensley Meulens 1989

Baseball was in the Olympics— from 1992 to 2008—and the U.S. won the gold medal once. Cuba won three times and South Korea, once.

Lithuania – Joe Kapustas 1933
Mexico – Mel Almada 1933
Puerto Rico Hi Bithorn 1942
Austria – Kurt Krieger 1949
Dominican Republic – Ozzie Virgil 1956
Japan – Masanori Murakami 1964
Nicaragua – Dennis Martinez 1976
Spain – Bryan Oelkers 1983
South Korea – Chan Ho Park 1994
Aruba – Gene Kingsale 1996
Belgium – Brian Lesher 1996
Philippines – Bobby Chouinard 1996
Taiwan – Chin-Feng Chen 2002
Guam – John Hattig 2006
Brazil – Yan Gomes 2012

WOMEN IN BASEBALL

Pro baseball is strictly men-only. Maybe that will change someday. But the numbers suggest otherwise.

There are thousands of girls playing organized baseball around the world. But hundreds of thousands more opt for softball instead. Why? Good question. It seems that softball was created as a "safer" alternative for girls in the 1970s and has stayed the default for registration ever since.

For a short time during and after World War II, women had their own professional league: the All-American Girls Professional Baseball League (AAGPBL). It folded after the 1954 season. Baseball fans were willing to accept women players during the war, but as gender roles changed back to pre-war expectations (men at jobs, women at home), the league fell out of favor.

1931

Seventeen year-old Jackie Mitchell strikes out the best Yankee hitters, Babe Ruth and Lou Gehrig, in an exhibition game. There is talk of signing her to a pro contract, but MLB Commissioner Kenesaw Mountain Landis decides baseball is "too strenuous" for women.

Things aren't any easier for women off the field.

To date, only a very few women have ever owned a major league baseball team. Marge Schott is the most famous. She was the owner of the Cincinnati Reds when the team won the World Series in 1990. There are no female coaches. Sue Falsone was the first female trainer. She worked for the Los Angeles Dodgers from 2011 to 2013.

Even announcing is mostly a man's world. In 1964, Betty Caywood became the first on-air reporter. She worked one month for the Kansas City Royals.

There's still only one woman in the broadcast booth. Susyn Waldman is the full-time color commentator for the New York Yankees. That's 1 woman out of 60 announcers. If that was a batting average, it would be terrible—.016!

1935

Kitty Burke, a fan of the Cincinnati Reds and a well-known entertainer, runs onto the field and grabs the bat during a game. She dares the pitcher, Daffy Dean, to throw a pitch. He does, and she hits the ball. She runs and is thrown out at first base. It is never recorded as an official hit, but no one had called time out, either, so Burke makes sure everyone knows her as the first woman to play in the big leagues. The Reds even give her a commemorative jersey.

1950

Kathryn Johnston is the first girl to play on an organized baseball team. She tucks her hair under her cap and says she is a boy. She does tell her coach eventually, and he lets her stay on the team.

WHO MAKES THE MAJORS?

Skill-testing question: There are 11 million kids playing baseball in North America. How many will make the "bigs"?

28

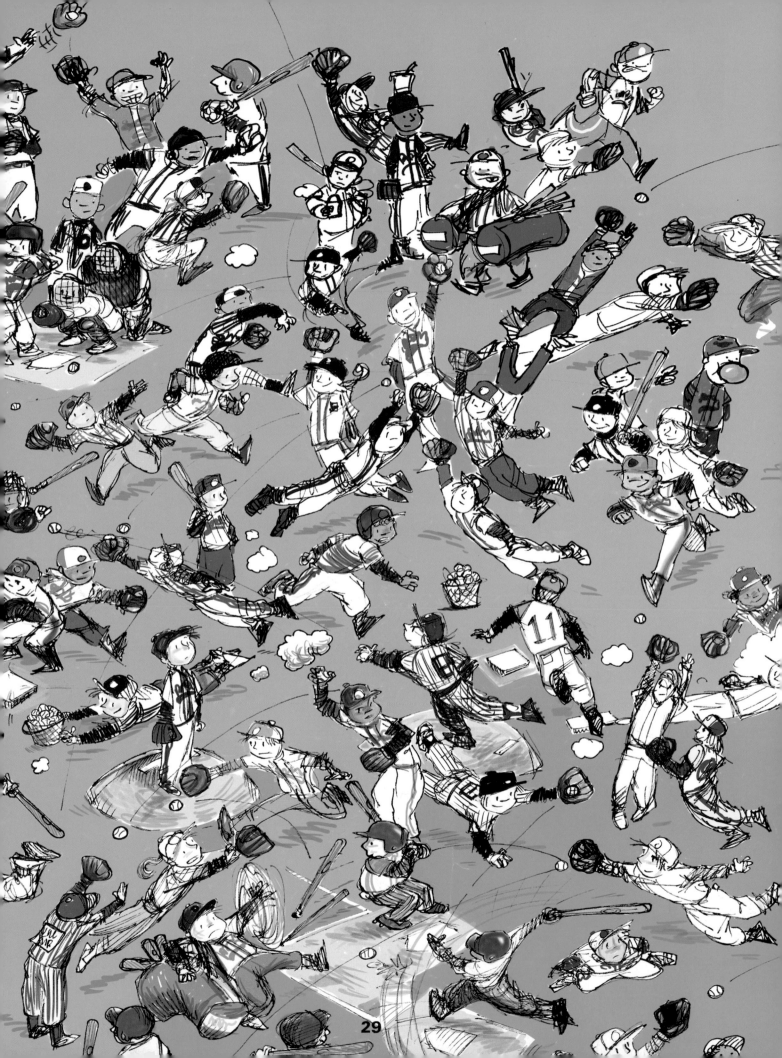

Answer:
Only about 800.

See how hard it is?

About **10,000** of those **11 million** will make it to the various levels of the minor leagues. So, the chances of making it one to three steps away from the majors is **1** in **1,100**.

But of those **10,000** minor leaguers, only about **800** will actually advance to the major leagues.

When all the math is done, those baseball-loving kids in North America have about a **1** in **14,000** chance of making it to "the Show."

And that **1** player? There's no guarantee that kid will have a *career* in the major leagues.

"The Show"– that's what baseball insiders call the major leagues.

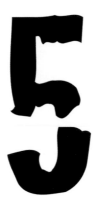

5

ONE EXPENSIVE HEADACHE

Lots of players miss time because they're sick and injured but never regain their spots. Wally Pipp is a good example. On June 2, 1925, Pipp came down with a headache during the Yankees game against the Washington Senators. He was replaced by a young player named Lou Gehrig. Gehrig went on to set the record for consecutive games played—2,130 in a row, starting on that day. Pipp never played for the Yankees again. He called it the "most expensive two aspirin" he ever took. (Pipp did play a few more years with Cincinnati, though.)

The average length of a baseball career is just five seasons. That's the average. What that means is that there are major leaguers who play for many more seasons, and major leaguers who play for many less. Every year dozens of players only suit up for a few games, or maybe get called up but never take the field or step up to the plate—and then spend the rest of their careers in the minor leagues.

Many players have played only one game, but Jimmy Boyle played only *one inning*, in 1926. He was a catcher called in for the ninth inning and never even got to bat. He retired after the game and became a famous restaurateur.

At the other extreme, first base player Cap Anson and pitcher Nolan Ryan both spent *27 years* playing at the major league level.

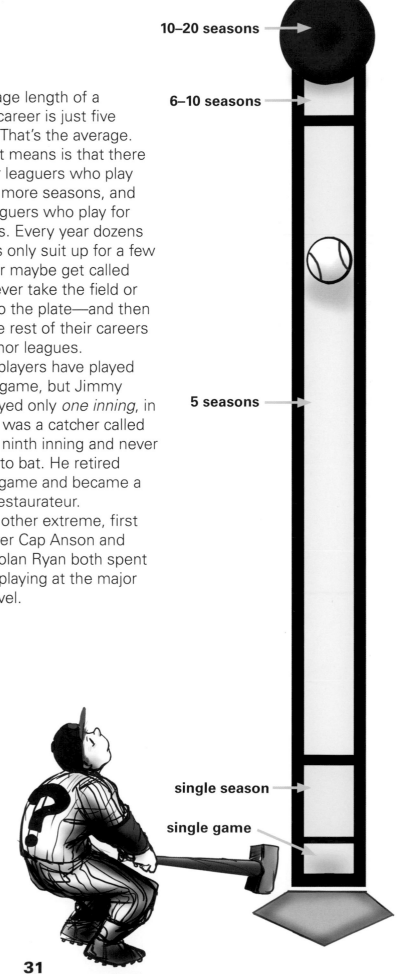

10–20 seasons

6–10 seasons

5 seasons

single season

single game

PITCHING

Baseball is a game of statistics. Owners love them, managers and coaches love them, and fans love them. Different stats are used to gauge the ability of batters and hitters.

Tom Hurler

A Cy Young–winning season would look something like Tom Hurler's stats. But what do they mean?

GS: games started

GP: games pitched. Tom is a starting pitcher, so he only pitches games that he starts. A relief pitcher could appear in many more games, sometimes 70-plus.

ER: earned runs—in other words, runs that score legitimately, not as a result of an error.

W: wins. Tom won 24 games, which makes him quite a pitcher! Twenty-plus is the gold standard. Denny McLain was the last pitcher to win 30 games, in 1968 with Detroit.

CY YOUNG
The award for best pitcher in the major leagues is named for him. Young was one of the greatest pitchers of all time. Beginning in 1890, he pitched 21 seasons, started 815 games (still a record), and won 511 games (also still a record).

Some pitchers will have S for saves. Mariano Rivera saved 652 games for the New York Yankees from 1995 to 2013. Francisco Rodriguez holds the single season record—62 in 2008, for Los Angeles.

L: losses. Tom's 5 losses to 24 wins gives him an incredible winning percentage. There are a few pitchers out there who compare. Detroit's Justin Verlander has won about 80% of the games he's pitched … so far.

BB: base on balls—also known as walks

ERA: earned run average—This is the average number of runs that Tom allows over nine innings—the length of a complete game. Tom pitched 251 innings. In order to get the number of "nine-inning games" that make up his season, you have to do math: 251/9 = 27.9. Tom gave up 67 earned runs. Divide the total earned runs by the number of nine-innings games and you get the average number of runs he gave up per nine innings—2.401433691756272. Round that to something that fits on a baseball card and you get an ERA of 2.40.

IP: innings pitched

H: hits allowed

```
10          TOM HURLER                    P
     PILLTOWN PITCHERS
     Ht: 6'1" Wt: 215 Bats: Left Throws: Right Home: Stitches, TX
     Drafted: 2010 1st round Free agent: 2018 Birthday: May 15th, 1994
```

MAJOR LEAGUE CAREER RECORD

YR	GS	GP	IP	ER	W	L	H	BB	ERA	WHIP	K
14	34	34	251	67	24	5	174	57	2.40	.920	250
TOTALS	34	34	251	67	24	5	174	57	2.40	.920	250

WHIP: walks and hits per innings pitched. Add Tom's hits (174) and walks (57) and you get 231. Divide that by the total number of innings Tom pitched for (251) and you get .920318725099602 (rounded to .920). That tells you that Tom has incredible pitch control—in other words, the ball goes where he wants it to go, and batters have a tough time hitting it. A really good WHIP is only one hit or walk every inning.

K was first used to designate a strikeout by Henry Chadwick, the inventor of the box score. He said K was the most recognized sound in the word.

K: strikeouts. Two hundred is considered top-notch. Tom had 250. That means he throws hard and accurately.

MESSING WITH YOUR BRAIN

Baseball seems simple. The pitcher stands on the mound. The pitcher throws a ball. The batter tries to hit the ball.

But things are rarely as simple as they seem, and in baseball, every pitch involves a network of possibilities.

Basically, the pitcher is trying to trick the batter's brain.

How?

Well, by throwing something the hitter doesn't expect, but also by mixing up the pitches.

It works like this.

B   A   S   E

How fast is a pitch? Say the word "baseball" at a normal speed. The pitcher lets go of the ball

What's a batter to do? He can try to predict what the pitcher will throw, so that he can adjust his swing to meet the ball.

But the pitcher further messes with the batter's brain by changing the "location" of the ball—where the ball is when it crosses the strike zone.

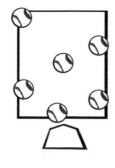

About 60% of all pitches are fastballs. The other four main pitches (curve, slider, breaking ball, cutter) are each thrown about 10% of the time. But pitchers will make their first pitch a fastball 80% of the time.

34

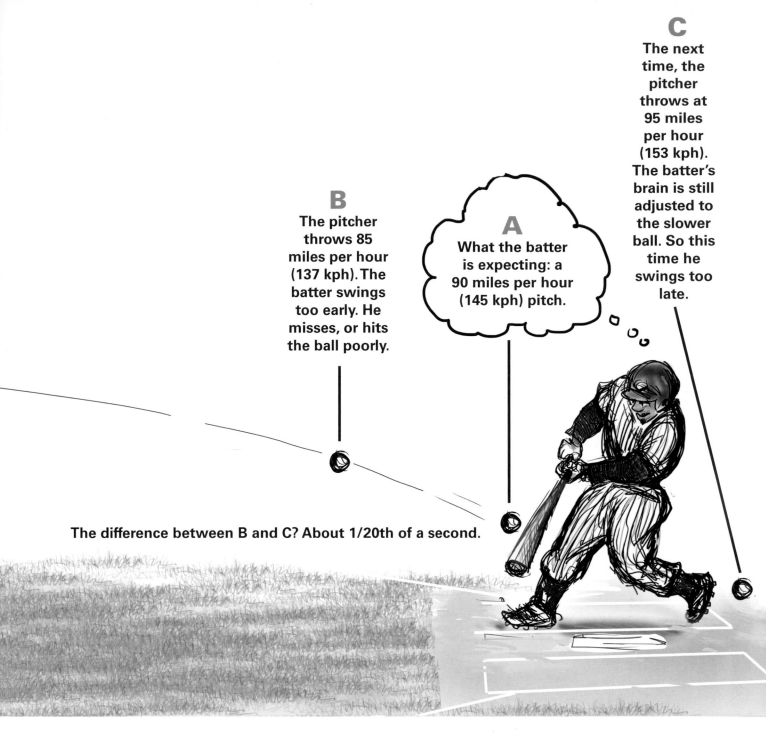

C
The next time, the pitcher throws at 95 miles per hour (153 kph). The batter's brain is still adjusted to the slower ball. So this time he swings too late.

B
The pitcher throws 85 miles per hour (137 kph). The batter swings too early. He misses, or hits the ball poorly.

A
What the batter is expecting: a 90 miles per hour (145 kph) pitch.

The difference between B and C? About 1/20th of a second.

B **A** **L** **L**

on the "b" and the ball hits the catcher's mitt anywhere from the second "a" to the last "l".

A knuckleball really messes with a batter's eyes and brains. It's pretty slow, but the ball hardly rotates, which means it wobbles in the air. (Normally, the rotation or "spin" on a ball makes it move more regularly down or sideways.)

Then there's the eephus pitch. The pitcher basically lobs the ball about 20 feet (6 meters) in the air and then the ball drops over the plate. It's so slow and abnormal that it's very hard for a batter to adjust. An eephus pitch takes almost a full second to reach the plate.

THE RISE OF THE RELIEVER

Pitching has changed tremendously since baseball's early days. Back then, pitchers stayed in the game for the full nine innings no matter what. Today, getting through a game is more of a team effort.

In 1916, the Phillies' Grover Alexander pitched an incredible 38 complete games. He faced 1,500 batters that season.

In 2013, David Price pitched four complete games for Tampa Bay. He faced about 750 batters.

Injuries are one big reason for the change.

These days, we're more aware of how much damage is done to the body by throwing a baseball over and over and over and over. To limit that wear and tear, managers usually limit a pitcher's "pitch count" to around 100 per game. It usually takes about 150 pitches to finish a game. This means a team's bullpen—which holds the other pitchers who can relieve the starting pitcher during the game—is much more important than it was in the past.

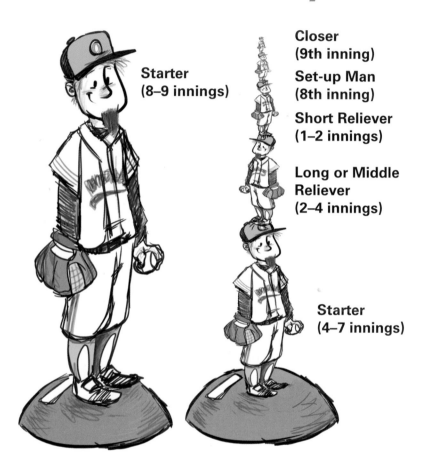

1916   Today

Starter (8–9 innings)

Closer (9th inning)
Set-up Man (8th inning)
Short Reliever (1–2 innings)
Long or Middle Reliever (2–4 innings)
Starter (4–7 innings)

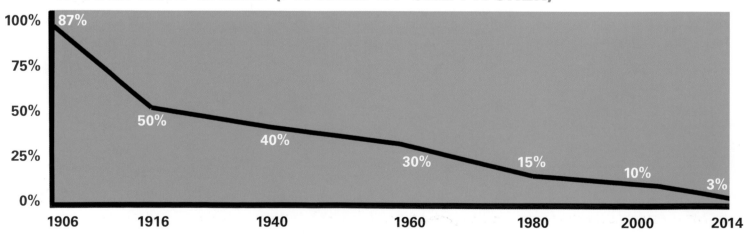

% COMPLETE GAMES (PITCHED BY ONE PITCHER)

87%	50%	40%	30%	15%	10%	3%
1906	1916	1940	1960	1980	2000	2014

THE HEIGHT OF THE MOUND

Tiny differences can have a huge impact in the game of baseball.

1968

16 inches (40.5 centimeters) avg

In **1968**, pitchers ruled over hitters like giants. Bob Gibson of the St. Louis Cardinals allowed just over 1 run every 9 innings (a 1.12 ERA). He pitched 13—yes, 13—shutouts! That year, 8 other pitchers had ERAs under 2.00.

In Boston, Carl Yastrzemski was the only American League (AL) batter to hit over .300 (.301). Only 5 players in the National League (NL) hit above .300. The batting average for the entire major leagues was .237—the lowest of all time.

Only 7 players hit 30 or more home runs.

1969

10 inches (25.5 centimeters)

In **1969**, everything changed. Officials shaved 6 inches (15 centimeters) off the top of the mound, and suddenly the pitchers didn't seem so huge.

The overall batting average jumped 10 points. Twenty-four players hit .300 or above. Seventeen hit 30 or more home runs. And not a single pitcher had an ERA under 2.00. San Francisco's Juan Marichal led the league with a 2.10.

NO RELIEF

There are some exceptions to the "shorter and more" rule. In 2013, San Francisco's Tim Lincecum stayed in for an entire game and threw an astonishing 148 pitches. He was on his way to a no-hitter when his pitch count started creeping up, and managers just don't take out a pitcher who might throw a no-hitter.

HITTING

Billy Beard's baseball card lists lots of biographical information (name, age, weight, etc.) and then the statistics for his career—year by year and cumulative. It tells you almost everything you need to know about him as a hitter.

Billy Beard

AB: at bats—The number of times a player was at the plate for either a hit or an out. A walk doesn't count as an at bat in the same way.

G: games played—There are 162 games in a standard season.

H: hits—150 is not bad; 200 hits is considered the gold standard.

2B: doubles

WHAT A CARD!

Serious collectors can pay millions for a rare baseball card.

The most famous card is the Honus Wagner T206 card. T206 refers to the card series that the American Tobacco Company released between 1909 and 1911. Only about a hundred cards were ever released, for free, inside the cigarette packs. Wagner was one of the best players of all time, but he asked the company to stop using his image on the cards. One story suggests he didn't want kids to buy cigarettes.

In 2013, a mint-condition T206 Wagner sold at auction for *more than $2 million*.

3B: triples

R: runs scored

RBI: runs batted in—This is how many times Billy has batted in either himself (with a home run) or other players.

SO: strikeouts—Billy strikes out about half as many times as he gets a hit. That's not bad. Mark Reynolds holds the record. He struck out 223 times in 2009, while playing for Arizona. He had 578 at bats that season and 150 hits.

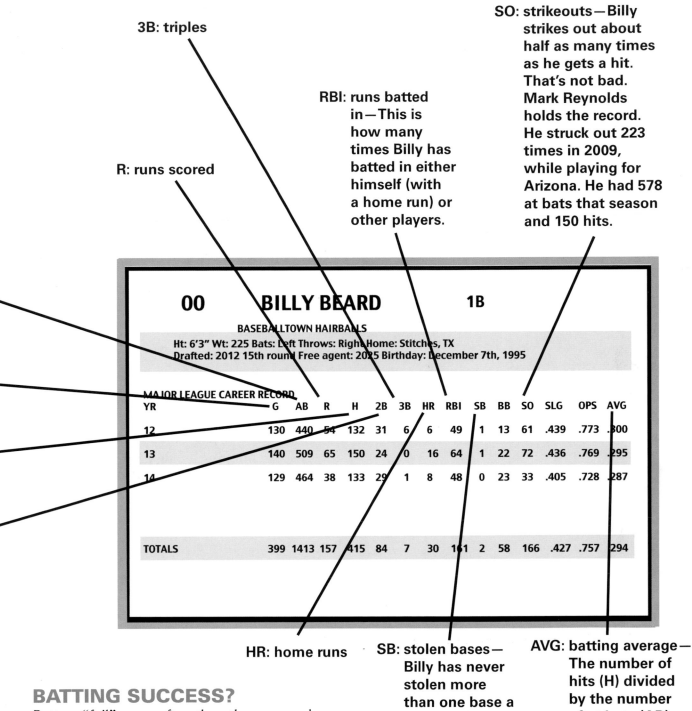

| 00 | BILLY BEARD | | | | | | | | | 1B | | | | |

BASEBALLTOWN HAIRBALLS

Ht: 6'3" Wt: 225 Bats: Left Throws: Right Home: Stitches, TX
Drafted: 2012 15th round Free agent: 2025 Birthday: December 7th, 1995

MAJOR LEAGUE CAREER RECORD

YR	G	AB	R	H	2B	3B	HR	RBI	SB	BB	SO	SLG	OPS	AVG
12	130	440	54	132	31	6	6	49	1	13	61	.439	.773	.300
13	140	509	65	150	24	0	16	64	1	22	72	.436	.769	.295
14	129	464	38	133	29	1	8	48	0	23	33	.405	.728	.287
TOTALS	399	1413	157	415	84	7	30	161	2	58	166	.427	.757	.294

HR: home runs

SB: stolen bases—Billy has never stolen more than one base a season. That's a sure sign he's not the fastest runner in the game.

AVG: batting average—The number of hits (H) divided by the number of at bats (AB). A .300 average is considered good. It means Billy gets a hit 3 of every 10 times at bat.

BATTING SUCCESS?

Batters "fail" more often than they succeed.

Ted Williams was the last batter to have an average of more than .400— .406 in 1941, playing for the Boston Red Sox. The Royals' George Brett hit .390 in 1980. Tony Gwynn was batting .394 for the San Diego Padres when the 1994 season was cut short by a strike.

The infamous Mendoza Line refers to Mario Mendoza, a player in the 1970s who could barely maintain a .200 average. He played defense well, so he kept his job. Players still refer to the .200 line as the difference between bad and mediocre.

This is just the tip of the stats revolution iceberg. For even more amazing stuff, check out pages 62 and 63.

BATTING BASICS

Hall-of-Famer Willie Stargell once described hitting like this: "They give you a round bat and they throw you a round ball and they tell you to hit it square." And you have to do that in a blink of an eye.

It takes a baseball about four-tenths of a second to reach home plate. In that blink of an eye, the batter has to make a number of decisions. Is it in the strike zone? Is it a ball? Is it coming in high or low? Fast or (relatively) slow?

How do batters manage to wait until the last possible millisecond to get it right? To hit the ball with the most force off the "sweet spot" of the bat?

The key is bat speed. The faster the batter swings, the longer he can wait to spot the ball.

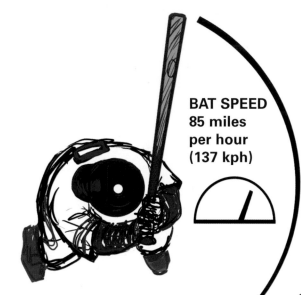

BAT SPEED
85 miles per hour (137 kph)

This swing takes less than half a second.

PITCH SPEED
90 mph (145 kph)

EXIT SPEED
100 miles per hour (161 kph)

Once the batter does have that ball in his sights, he wants to bring the bat through the strike zone with as much force *and* speed as possible. The faster the swing, the faster the ball comes off the bat. This is sometimes known as the "exit speed" of the ball.

Cincinnati's Heinie Groh used a 41-ounce (1.16-kg) bat with an abnormally large barrel during his career in the early 1900s. He called it a "bottle bat." He was a very good hitter, but had very small hands, so the bat worked for him.

BALANCING ACT

A fast bat is best, but a fast heavy bat is better than a fast light bat. Most hitters try to swing as heavy a bat as they can as fast as they can. A heavy bat will hit the ball farther if it's swung at the same speed as a lighter bat, but at what point is the bat too heavy for the batter to swing fast?

That is different for each hitter. Most players use bats somewhere around 30 to 36 ounces (.850 to 1.02 kg). When he was young, Babe Ruth once used a bat that weighed more than 50 ounces (more than 3 pounds, or almost 1.5 kg). He later chose with a bat closer to 40 ounces (1.13 kg) and then 35 ounces (just under a kilogram).

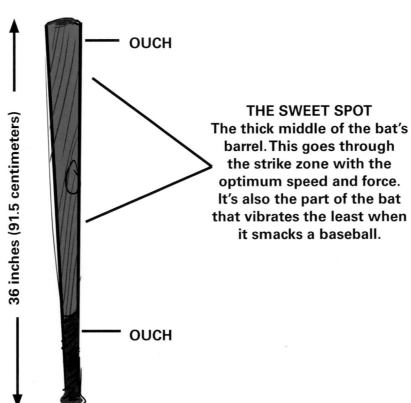

36 inches (91.5 centimeters)

OUCH

OUCH

THE SWEET SPOT
The thick middle of the bat's barrel. This goes through the strike zone with the optimum speed and force. It's also the part of the bat that vibrates the least when it smacks a baseball.

OUCH!

Sometimes batters will "crowd the plate"—lean in right over it to get a better position. They risk getting hit by the pitch, but that does get them on base, so some use it as a strategy. Hughie Jennings, who played from 1891 to 1918, was hit a record 287 times.

HOME RUNS AND THE BAMBINO

Go to a game today, and you are very likely to see at least one home run. That's not the way the game started.

A hundred years ago, there was no such thing as a "power hitter." Everyone played what is often referred to as "small ball." Batters would aim for singles, doubles, or (if lucky) triples.

Home runs happened, but they were rare. Gavvy Cravath led the majors in 1915 with 24 home runs. Braggo Roth led the American League with seven.

Then Babe Ruth happened.

Ruth had been one of the best pitchers in baseball for his first couple of seasons with Boston. But a pitcher doesn't play every day, and the Babe really liked to hit the ball—and hit it a long way. So, he started batting more and pitching less.

Look at his home run record after that:

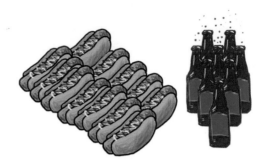

Ruth was no health freak. He once missed a bunch of games because of indigestion. He'd eaten a dozen hot dogs and guzzled eight sodas between games.

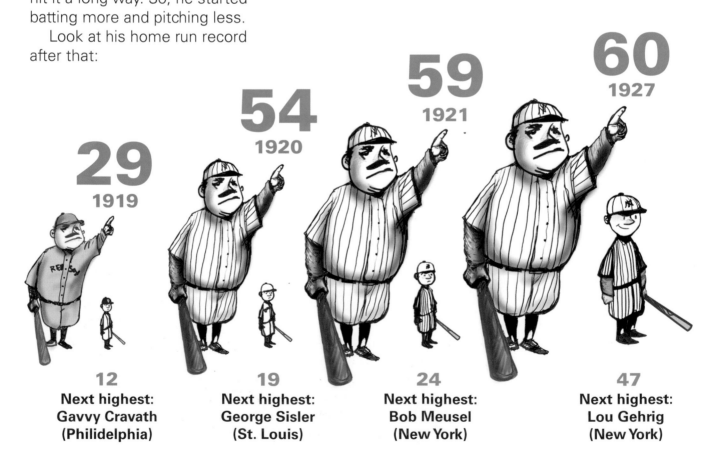

29
1919

12
Next highest:
Gavvy Cravath
(Philidelphia)

54
1920

19
Next highest:
George Sisler
(St. Louis)

59
1921

24
Next highest:
Bob Meusel
(New York)

60
1927

47
Next highest:
Lou Gehrig
(New York)

Chasing the Bambino

Those 60 homers remained the record for 34 long years. Roger Maris hit 61 home runs in 1961. But there's an * next to that achievement.

After Ruth, the home run became a huge part of the game. Now, every team relies on the homer as part of its strategy for winning.

SINGLE-SEASON RECORDS

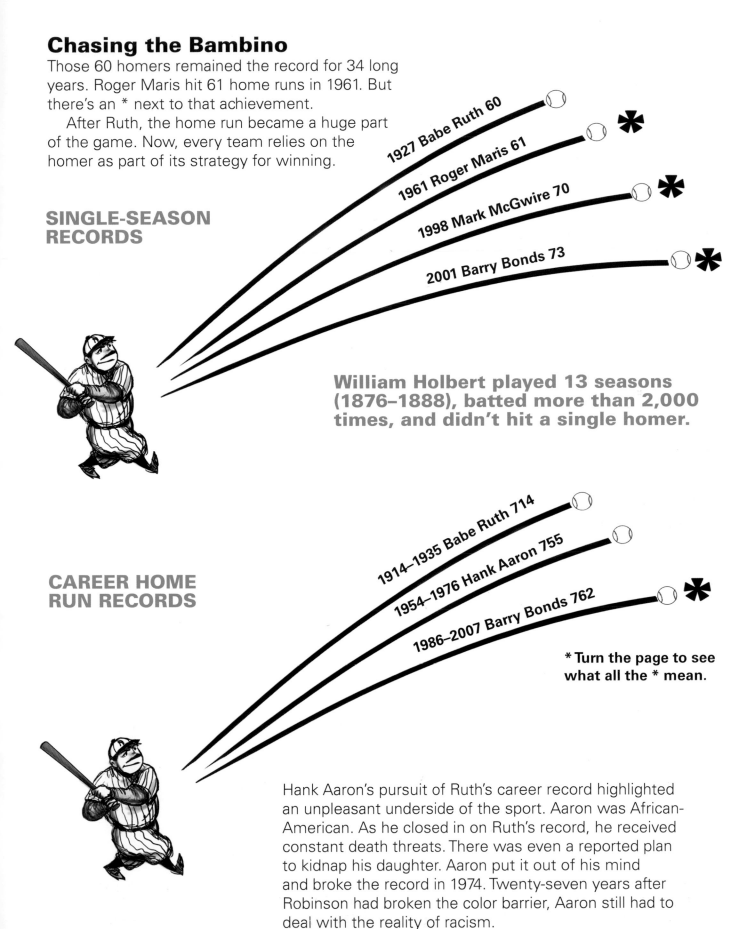

1927 Babe Ruth 60

1961 Roger Maris 61 *

1998 Mark McGwire 70 *

2001 Barry Bonds 73 *

William Holbert played 13 seasons (1876–1888), batted more than 2,000 times, and didn't hit a single homer.

CAREER HOME RUN RECORDS

1914–1935 Babe Ruth 714

1954–1976 Hank Aaron 755

1986–2007 Barry Bonds 762 *

* Turn the page to see what all the * mean.

Hank Aaron's pursuit of Ruth's career record highlighted an unpleasant underside of the sport. Aaron was African-American. As he closed in on Ruth's record, he received constant death threats. There was even a reported plan to kidnap his daughter. Aaron put it out of his mind and broke the record in 1974. Twenty-seven years after Robinson had broken the color barrier, Aaron still had to deal with the reality of racism.

*THERE'S MORE TO THE STORY

An asterisk (*) means there's more to the story, and that's definitely true when it comes to breaking Babe Ruth's home run records.

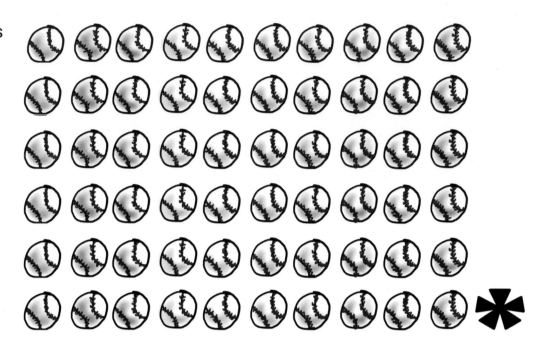

Roger Maris was the first to break the record for home runs in a single season. In 1961 he hit **61** for the New York Yankees.

But Maris received incredible abuse from baseball fans, many of whom felt he wasn't worthy of breaking Ruth's record. Maris had been a pretty good hitter, but he wasn't the flamboyant superstar Ruth had been. Maris was so stressed at points in the season that he'd even started losing his hair.

When Maris did manage to hit **61** home runs, league Commissioner Ford Frick (who had been a friend of Ruth's) put an asterisk next to the record. Why? He argued that it had taken Maris **162** games to reach the mark. Ruth had done it in **154** games—eight fewer. Maris was always bitter about the way he'd been treated.

 In 1998, two hitters broke Maris's record: Mark McGwire and Sammy Sosa. McGwire ended his season with **70**, while Sosa had **66**. McGwire later admitted to using performance-enhancing drugs. Lots of people felt there should have been an asterisk next to that record as well, but it was soon broken.

There is a home run ball in the Baseball Hall of Fame with an asterisk carved right into the leather. The ball was hit by Barry Bonds of the San Francisco Giants. Bonds broke the single-season home run record *and* Aaron's career home run record. But Bonds's record was shadowed by drug scandal.

When Bonds hit home run number **756** (breaking Aaron's record), a fan caught the ball, then sold it to baseball fanatic Marc Ecko for more than **$750,000**.

Ecko held an online vote, asking what he should do with the ball. Fans voted to have the ball marked with an asterisk—to mark what they saw as a dubious moment in baseball history. Ecko obliged. Then he donated the ball to the Hall.

The shadow of that * has never left Bonds. His career numbers should make him an automatic Hall of Fame player, but the reports of banned-drug use have kept him from getting enough votes to be elected.

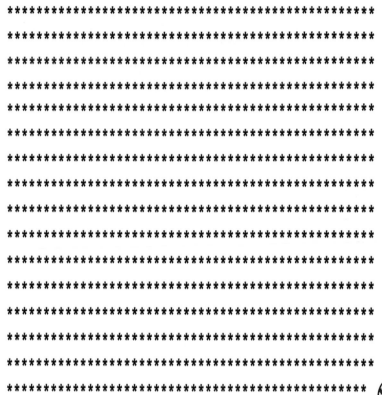

Other notable *'s

 Pete Rose holds the career record for hits, but has been kept out of the Hall of Fame for admitting that he gambled on baseball.

 The St. Louis Browns were one of the most hapless franchises in baseball history, but they won the 1944 World Series. Why an *? Because of World War II, the major leagues lost many talented players and so the 1944 victory is often considered a bit of a fluke.

868

Sadaharu Oh holds the all-time pro record for home runs. He hit 868 during his 21-year career with the Yomiuri Giants of the Japanese League.

LONG GAMES

Baseball games have been known to go on … and on. If the score is tied after nine innings, the teams just keep playing until someone ends an inning in the lead. This has led to some marathon games.

26

25

9

A game can (theoretically) go on forever

1920: longest game ever, Boston vs. Brooklyn, declared a 1–1 once it got dark and became impossible to continue

1984: longest game ever with a winner, Chicago vs. Milwaukee, 7–6 (it lasted 8 hours and 6 minutes, also a record!)

Length of a typical game

INNINGS

Nine-inning games can be pretty long too. In 2006, the Orioles beat the Yankees 14–11 in the longest nine-inning game ever played—a marathon **4 hours and 45 minutes**.

Okay, so maybe *some* baseball games can be boring … especially if they end five hours past your bedtime!

MINOR LEAGUE, MAJOR GAME

In 1981, the Pawtucket and Rochester teams played a very unusual 33-inning game in AAA league baseball. The first 32 innings were played on April 18 and 19, and the players were pooped. So they stopped and then played what turned out to be the final inning in June. Pawtucket won 3—2.

The shortest nine-inning game was just 51 minutes long. The New York Giants beat the Philadelphia Phillies 6–1 in 1919.

1950

Today

Overall, games are a lot longer now than they used to be.

Fifty years ago, a baseball game averaged a little more than two hours. Today they average just under three hours. But teams like the New York Yankees and Boston Red Sox average *over* three hours a game.

Why?

Commercial breaks for TV are part of the reason. They go a little longer than a normal break in between innings.

Also, players take frequent breaks to adjust their equipment. New York and Boston use them as part of their strategy to upset the opposing pitcher's rhythm. When Jonny Gomes played for Boston, he would tip his hat as many as five times between pitches and adjust each of his batting gloves … every time.

There are more pitcher changes in today's game, and each one adds a few minutes to the clock.

And there's music. Almost all teams now use little bits of music to introduce players.

It all adds up.

Major league baseball has started a commission to look at speeding up the games.

ZZZZzzzzzzzzzzzzzzzzz

Mike Hargrove was one of the first players to use the strategy of slowing down the game. He even earned the nickname "the human rain delay" because he added so much time to each time at bat.

SIZE

Have baseball players gotten bigger? Yes. Babe Ruth was a big guy—6 feet 2 inches (1.88 meters) and about 215 pounds (97.5 kilograms). Among his many nicknames were the Big Fellow, the Big Bam, and the Behemoth of Bust. Notice how often BIG is featured. He was huge for his day.

1927

Ruth's Yankee teammates averaged 5 feet 9 inches (1.75 meters) and 177 pounds (80 kilograms). But today, Ruth's height and weight are almost the average for a major league player.

Today

The 2013 Yankees averaged 6 feet 1 inch (1.85 meters) and 205 pounds (93 kilograms).

The growth trend in baseball players is also true of the human species as a whole, especially in Western countries. A century ago, the average North American male was about 5 feet 6 inches (1.68 meters). Today, the average is around 5 feet 10 inches (1.78 meters). The average height for a woman is about 5 feet 6 inches (1.68 meters). Better nutrition and health care are big factors in our increasing size.

Pitcher Jon Rauch is the tallest player in history at 6 feet 11 inches (2.11 meters).

Eddie Gaedel was the smallest. He only played for one at bat, in 1951. He walked on four pitches. The number on his jersey, which is now in the Hall of Fame, was 1/8.

Walter Young is possibly the heaviest player of all time. He weighed around 320 pounds (145 kilograms).

3 feet 7 inches (1.09 meters)

Eddie Gaedel

AGE AND LONGEVITY

AGE

42

Satchel Paige is the oldest rookie to ever suit up in the major leagues, at age 42 (or possibly older—birth records were a little sketchy back then). He had played for decades in the Negro Leagues but he was finally allowed to play in the major leagues, so he debuted with the Cleveland Indians in 1948.

Paige also holds the record for the oldest player of all time. He retired in 1965 at the age of 59 (or so).

16

Frank "Piggy" Ward was just a month past his 16th birthday when he became the youngest non-pitcher rookie in 1883.

15

Joe Nuxhall was just 15 (and 10 months) when he broke in with Cincinnati in 1944. He pitched only one inning and gave up five runs. He was sent back to the minors after the game, but he never gave up. Nuxhall was back in the majors in 1952 and stayed there until 1966. He became an announcer after that and worked for another 37 years.

LONG CAREERS

5

Two players had careers that spanned five decades. Nick Altrock played part-time from 1898 to 1933, and Minnie Minoso played from 1949 to 1980. Minoso originally retired in 1964, but he staged short comebacks in 1976 and 1980.

27

Nolan Ryan and Cap Anson tie for the longest career of all time. They each played 27 seasons—Nolan from 1966–1993 and Anson from 1871–1897.

37

Bruce Froemming was an umpire for 37 full seasons, from 1971 to 2007. Bill Klem also umpired for 37 seasons, but his last year was part-time.

35

Joe West umpired his 35th season in 2014. He was 61 at the time. Froemming was 68 when he retired. Will West break Froemming's record? It seems likely!

53

Connie Mack was a manager for 53 years. That's 7,755 games! He retired in 1950, at the age of 87.

UNBREAKABLE RECORDS?

There are records broken and set almost every season, but some of baseball's best seem unbreakable.

GAMES PLAYED

Pete Rose, **3,562** (1963–1986)

Carl Yastrzemski, **3,308** (1961–83)

CONSECUTIVE GAMES

Cal Ripken, **2,632** (May 30, 1982 to September 19, 1998)

Lou Gehrig, **2,130** (June 1, 1925 to April 30, 1939)

Lou Gehrig was forced to end his streak after being diagnosed with amyotrophic lateral sclerosis (ALS), a disease that attacks the nervous system. To this day it is often referred to as "Lou Gehrig's disease."

HITTING STREAKS

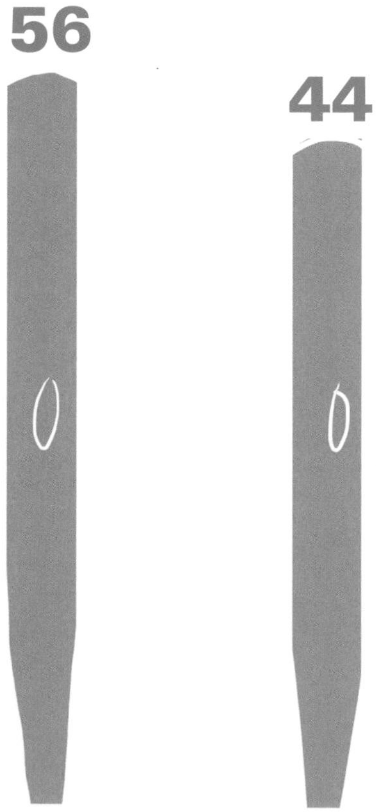

56

44

0–0
Johnny Vander Meer pitched back-to-back no-hitters in 1938. No one has even come close since.

Joe DiMaggio (1941) hit in 56 straight games.

Pete Rose (1978) and Wee Willie Keeler (1897) hit in 44 straight games.

HITS IN A SEASON

262
Ichiro Suzuki (2004)

257
George Sisler (1920)

STEALS

Rickey Henderson, **1,406** (1979–2003)

Lou Brock, **938** (1961–1979)

STRAIGHT WINS

The New York Giants, **26** (1916)

The Oakland Athletics, **20** (2002)

WORLD SERIES

The New York Yankees, **5** in a row (1949–1953)

The Yankees again! **4** straight (1936–1939)

CAREER STRIKEOUTS

5,714

4,875

Nolan Ryan

Randy Johnson

FUTILITY
The Chicago Cubs haven't won a World Series since 1908. Cleveland last won in 1948.

FREAK INJURIES

Baseball might seem like a pretty safe sport. There are few collisions and no (legal) tackles. But it's amazing how many ways players can find to get injured … on and off the field.

Kendry Morales once hit a grand slam (a home run with the bases loaded) to help his team, the Los Angeles Angels, win a big game. His teammates were so excited, they mobbed him at home plate. He jumped in the air, landed in the middle of the crowd, and broke his leg. Morales missed the rest of that season *and* the next.

Detroit Tiger **Joel Zumaya** missed a whole series in the 2006 play offs with a wrist injury. It turned out he'd strained it playing *Guitar Hero*.

Dwight Gooden once missed a game after getting hit by a golf club, swung by Vince Coleman in the New York Mets clubhouse.

Infielder **Bret Barbarie** once got injured making nachos. He did wash his hands after cutting chilies, but there was still some chili oil left behind and when he put in his contacts, he burned his eyes.

Milwaukee's **Steve Sparks** missed most of spring training in 1994. He dislocated his shoulder trying to rip a phone book in half.

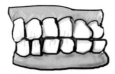

Clarence Blethen was pulled from a Red Sox game after biting himself on the butt. Each time he played, Blethen would remove his false teeth and stick them in his back pocket. He hit a double, forgot about the teeth, and slid into second. The teeth sank right in.

Tyler Colvin had to go to hospital after getting stabbed by a bat. He was standing on third, watching his Chicago Cubs teammate Wellington Castillo bat. Castillo took a swing and the bat shattered. A shard flew straight at Colvin and stabbed him in the chest.

Vince Coleman missed the entire 1985 World Series after he got caught up in the rain tarp and wrenched his leg.

SUSPENSIONS

Many players have been suspended for breaking the rules of the game. Gambling is a real no-no, as are banned drugs. Lifetime bans are more common than you think.

Ever heard of the Black Sox? Cincinnati won the 1919 World Series, but reports later emerged that some members of the losing Chicago White Sox had accepted bribes to throw the games—that's right, lose the games *on purpose*. Eight players were banned from baseball for life. Buck Weaver didn't take a bribe, but he knew about the scheme, and that was enough to get him banned.

Milwaukee's **Ryan Braun** is a great hitter, but reports have swirled for years about him and performance-enhancing drugs. The MLB investigated and Braun was suspended in 2013 for **65 games**. He lost more than **$3 million** in salary.

The Yankees' **Alex Rodriguez** has also been implicated in banned-drug use. He was banned for the entire 2014 season. That's **162 games** (and a lost salary of **$22 million**).

Three positive drug tests equal an automatic lifetime ban.

Pete Rose was one of the greatest players in history, but he also liked to gamble. After retiring he became a manager. It turned out that he bet thousands of dollars on baseball, and even on his own team. He was banned for life from baseball, and despite his many records, is not eligible for the Hall of Fame.

Alex Sánchez was the first player suspended for the use of performance-enhancing drugs. In 2005, while playing for the Tampa Bay Devil Rays, he was barred from **10 games**. That was the maximum penalty for a first-time offense. Many felt the penalty was too light, so the MLB later upped the limit.

When the Dodgers' **Manny Ramirez** tested positive for banned drugs in 2009, he was suspended for **50 games**. A couple of years later he tested positive again; this time, the penalty was **100 games**.

SALARIES

Sportcasts are full of stories about athletes getting paid millions of dollars. But it wasn't always like that.

Baseball has seen a huge rise in salaries over the last hundred years. It took a while.

From the beginning of the pro game until about 40 years ago, teams basically owned their players for life. Each contract contained a clause that reserved their rights. This was called the Reserve Clause Era.

Then, in 1969, Curt Flood of the St. Louis Cardinals challenged the reserve clause. He lost, but players eventually won the right to become free agents. Flood never earned more than $100,000 and was chased out of the game by 1971. By 1975, players were free to sign with any team they wanted. The following year, free agency really took off. Teams began to bid against each other for the best players, and have been bidding ever since.

Notice how fast salaries rose once players could ask teams to bid for their services.

The highest paid player in Japan makes about 400 to 600 million yen ($5 to $7 million) a year. The average player earns much lower, between $50,000 and $100,000.

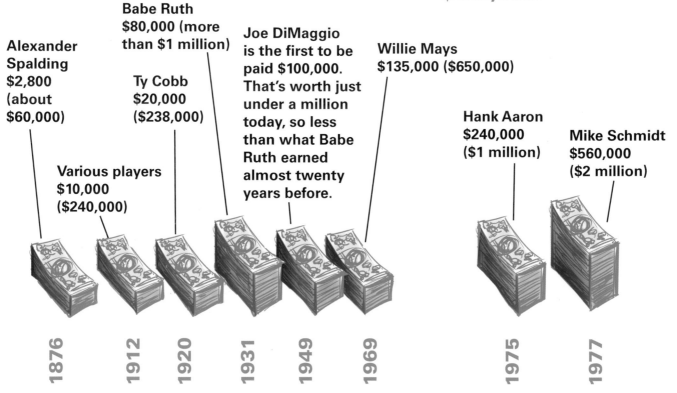

Alexander Spalding $2,800 (about $60,000)

Various players $10,000 ($240,000)

Babe Ruth $80,000 (more than $1 million)

Ty Cobb $20,000 ($238,000)

Joe DiMaggio is the first to be paid $100,000. That's worth just under a million today, so less than what Babe Ruth earned almost twenty years before.

Willie Mays $135,000 ($650,000)

Hank Aaron $240,000 ($1 million)

Mike Schmidt $560,000 ($2 million)

1876 1912 1920 1931 1949 1969   1975 1977

RESERVE CLAUSE ERA   **START OF FREE AGENT ERA**

(Amounts in brackets equal approximate equivalent in 2014 dollars.)

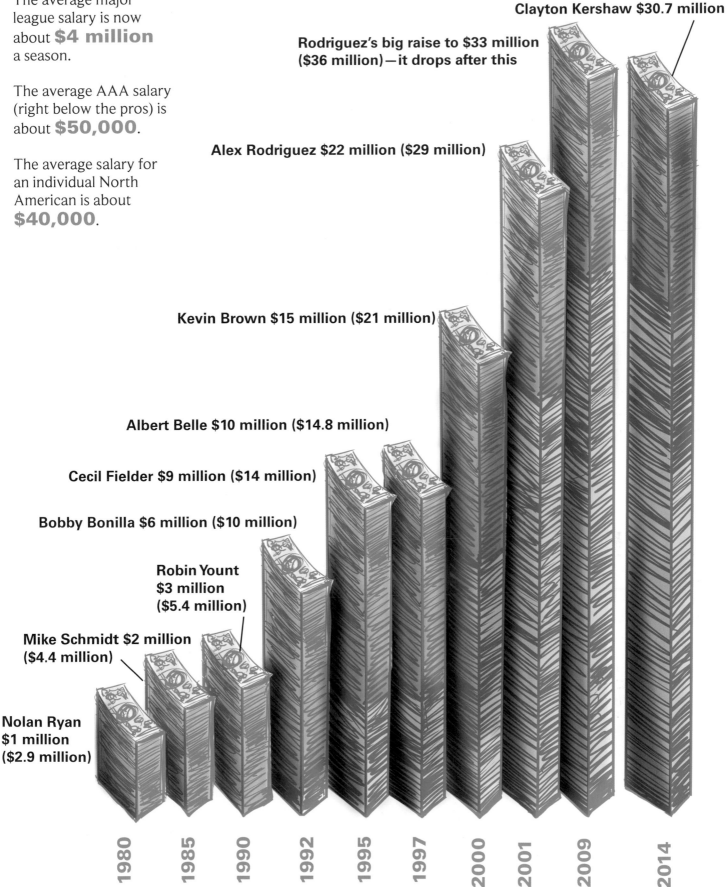

The average major league salary is now about **$4 million** a season.

The average AAA salary (right below the pros) is about **$50,000**.

The average salary for an individual North American is about **$40,000**.

Clayton Kershaw $30.7 million

Rodriguez's big raise to $33 million ($36 million)—it drops after this

Alex Rodriguez $22 million ($29 million)

Kevin Brown $15 million ($21 million)

Albert Belle $10 million ($14.8 million)

Cecil Fielder $9 million ($14 million)

Bobby Bonilla $6 million ($10 million)

Robin Yount $3 million ($5.4 million)

Mike Schmidt $2 million ($4.4 million)

Nolan Ryan $1 million ($2.9 million)

1980   1985   1990   1992   1995   1997   2000   2001   2009   2014

FREE AGENCY TAKES OFF

LISTENING AND WATCHING

Baseball used to be watched in fields and parks across the world, live. Then radio and TV started bringing the games to fans. Now, most people watch or listen to games at home.

The first radio broadcast of a big league game was in 1921, between Pittsburgh and Philly. (Pittsburgh won.) The first televised games were in 1939, between Brooklyn and Cincinnati. Each team won a game in a doubleheader.

Oddly, even as the total number of people watching baseball has gone up, the World Series has gone down in TV ratings—in other words, a smaller proportion of TV watchers are watching. There are more things to watch on TV today, so only diehard baseball fans and fans of the teams involved are guaranteed to watch.

HOW TO CATCH A GAME— THEN AND NOW

450 million

LEGEND:
Attendance ▬▬▬
Listeners ▬▬▬
Viewers ▬▬▬

74 million

6 million

1914　　1921　　1939　　2014

WORLD SERIES WATCHERS

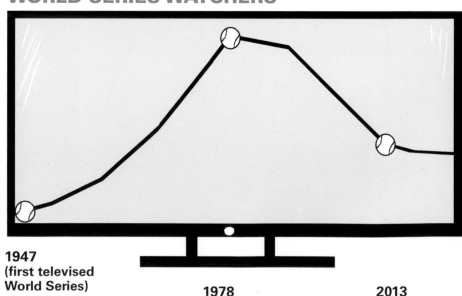

44 million
(Yankees beat L.A.)

15 million
(Boston beat St. Louis)

4 million
(Yankees beat Brooklyn)

1947
(first televised World Series)　　1978　　2013

56

With so many people watching and listening, it's no wonder the people who call the games become part of the fabric of their teams. Here are some long-time sportscasters and their records:

Vin Scully has called games for 65 seasons for the Dodgers, first in Brooklyn and then in LA, after the team moved in 1958. And (as of publication) he's still going!

Ernie Harwell broadcast for 54 years, 42 of them with Detroit (1960–2002). A trade kickstarted his career in 1948—Brooklyn wanted him as a broadcaster, but Harwell's minor league team (Atlanta) demanded a player in return. They got minor league catcher Cliff Dapper.

Harry Caray worked for 42 years. He broadcast more than 6,000 games in a row.

Red Barber worked 33 seasons for the Yankees, Dodgers, and Reds (1934–1966).

4,306
Number of games Toronto's **Tom Cheek** called before illness forced him to quit in 2004.

5,000+
The minor league team the Toledo Mud Hens believe their announcer—**Jim Weber**—holds the record for most games in a row with the same team. He hasn't missed a game since 1975, covering more than 5,000 so far!

ON THE MOVE

One hundred years ago, most teams were located in the eastern United States. Travel times between games were pretty short. Today's players spend half their games at home and half on the road. And depending on where "home" is, the road can be *looooooooooong.*

50,000 miles (80,467 kilometers)
Teams on the west coast travel the most per season. Seattle and Oakland players travel back and forth across the country for almost every series. They are the farthest from all the other teams, so that makes sense. But it might be one of the reasons why Seattle has never won a World Series, and Oakland hasn't won since 1989.

30,000 miles (48,280 kilometers)
Teams on the east coast travel for games in the west, but are otherwise pretty close to their opponents.

25,000 miles (40,234 kilometers)
Teams in the middle of the continent have it the easiest. Teams such as Cincinnati, Cleveland, Detroit, and Kansas City travel about half as much as their west coast rivals.

Travel can be even more tiring for the minor leaguers. The major league players travel on luxury planes with lots of spacious seats to and from their "away games". Minor leaguers travel by bus. They often pack their own equipment, and stay in pretty normal motels or hotels.

There can be a lot of family stress for minor leaguers as well. Major league players can afford to have their families live in the team's home city. Minor leaguers travel to wherever the jobs are, and can be moved up and down to different levels, in completely different cities, at a moment's notice.

Sometimes teams do more than travel—they move.

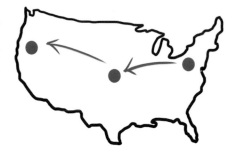

The Oakland A's (short for Athletics) were once the Philadelphia Athletics (1901–1954) and then the Kansas City Athletics (1955–1967).

The Baltimore Orioles started off as the St. Louis Browns (1902–1953), who were originally the Milwaukee Brewers (1901).

Washington might have the strangest history.
There have been four different Washington teams.
The current Washington Nationals were once the Montreal Expos (1969–2004).
The Washington Senators before that (1961–1971) are now the Texas Rangers.
The Washington Senators before that (1901–1960) are now the Minnesota Twins.
The original Washington Senators (1891–1899) folded.

Players move from team to team all the time.

1 FOR 1
Max Flack and Cliff Heathcote were traded for each other halfway through a doubleheader in 1922. They just exchanged jerseys.

2 IN 1!
In 1982 Joel Youngblood played a day game with the New York Mets in Chicago. During that game, he was traded to Montreal. He caught a flight to his new team's night game in Philadelphia and got there in time to play!

13
Octavio Dotel holds the record for most teams in a career—13.

CHAMPIONSHIPS

Each year a new team is "crowned" world champion by winning the World Series. But it's not really a "world" series at all. Only teams from the major leagues—the American League and the National League—in the United States and Canada can compete.

Which team has been crowned the most? The New York Yankees by far.

27
New York Yankees

11
St. Louis Cardinals

9
Oakland Athletics
(5 in Philadelphia,
4 in Oakland)

8
Boston Red Sox

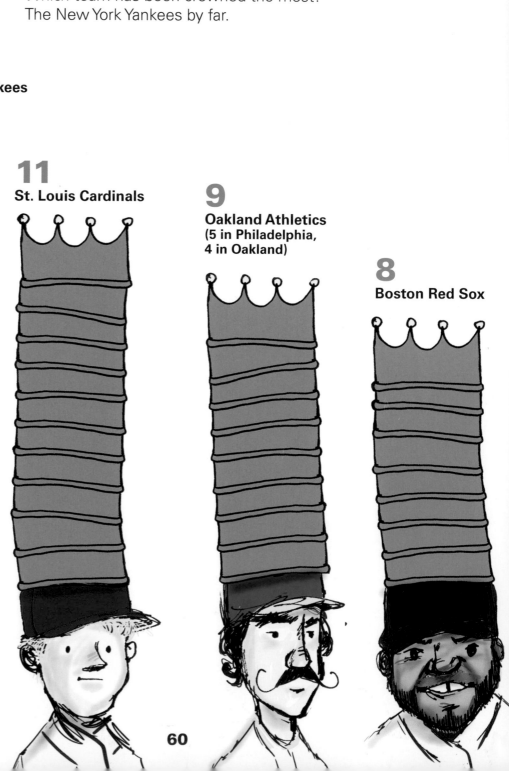

Eight relatively young teams have never won the World Series. Of those, the Texas Rangers have the longest stretch without a win. The team was founded in 1960 in Washington, D.C., and later moved to Texas.

OTHER SPORTS HAVE HAD DYNASTIES SIMILAR TO THE YANKEES.

6

The Pittsburgh Steelers have won 6 Super Bowls for football.

11

Manchester United has won 11 FA Cups for soccer.

8

San Francisco Giants (5 in New York, 3 in San Francisco)

6

L.A. Dodgers (1 in Brooklyn, 5 in Los Angeles)

24

The Montreal Canadiens have won 24 Stanley Cups for hockey.

17

The Boston Celtics have won 17 NBA titles for basketball.

RISE OF THE NEW STATS

Statistics have been gaining more and more importance in baseball. Can't play the game? Study math and you could still have a baseball career.

Canadian Bill James is the leader of the revolution. In the 1970s he started using statistical analysis to get a better picture of how the game actually worked. He found that some time-honored ideas about stealing bases, intentionally walking batters, and so on, didn't work as well as people thought.

He and others challenged the idea that a high batting average (such as .300) was the only good indicator of a player's value. They showed that a hitter who got on base with a combination of hits *and* walks could be just as valuable.

This has led to a revolution in the ways players are evaluated. Many teams now hire "stats geeks" or have what they call a "baseball analytics expert" on their staff.

Back when James started doing his research, no teams hired statisticians. Today at least 15 teams have hired or consult with stats experts. And that number continues to rise. James himself is an advisor with Boston.

The Society for American Baseball Research (SABR) has been at the forefront of looking at baseball using mathematics and statistics. Baseball analysts even use the term "Sabermetrics" to describe this way of critiquing the game.

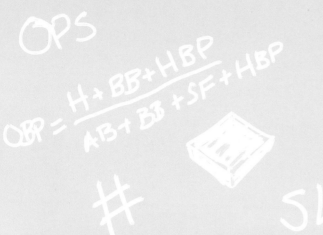

Economist Earnshaw Cook wrote a book in the 1960s called *Percentage Baseball* that looked at numbers and baseball. It interested some fans, but didn't gain wide acceptance.

The book *Moneyball* (which was eventually made into a movie) really launched this stats revolution into the mainstream. The book chronicles Oakland manager Billy Beane and his use of stats such as on-base percentage (OBP) to judge a player's value. He turned the Oakland A's into a contender by picking players that other teams undervalued with the traditional stats.

Today, there are lots of popular stats used to try and measure a player's value. These stats use many of the same terms found on pages 32–33 and 38–39.

OBP:

On-base percentage adds hits and walks and hits by pitch together to come up with how often, on average, a player gets on base.

$$OBP = \frac{H + BB + HBP}{AB + BB + SF + HBP}$$

SLG:

Slugging percentage is the total bases a player hits for, divided by the number of at bats. It's seen as a better indication of a player's power than just average or home runs on their own.

$$SLG = \frac{(1B) + (2B \times 2) + (3B \times 3) + (HR \times 4)}{AB}$$

OPS:

On-base percentage plus slugging is seen as an even better indicator of a player's overall value as a hitter. It takes all the bases a player gets to, including how many times a player was hit by a pitch and the number of times the player hit a sacrifice fly (a fly ball that scores a run, even though the batter is out.)

THE GROWTH OF ... EVERYTHING!

Baseball's popularity has always gone in waves. Teams have been born and have died. Other sports have taken over the title of "America's Pastime." But baseball has continued to grow in so many ways.

GAMES AND PLAYOFFS

1876
56–70 GAMES
0 PLAYOFFS
1 LEAGUE (NATIONAL)

1901
140 GAMES
0 PLAYOFFS
2 LEAGUES (AMERICAN AND NATIONAL)

1903
140 GAMES
1 PLAYOFF ROUND:
1st WORLD SERIES
(BOSTON OVER PITTSBURGH 5-3)*

1904
154 GAMES
1 PLAYOFF ROUND:
WORLD SERIES*

1962
162 GAMES
1 PLAYOFF ROUND:
WORLD SERIES

1969
162 GAMES
2 PLAYOFF ROUNDS:
AL/NL CHAMPIONSHIP SERIES*
WORLD SERIES

1994
162 GAMES
3 PLAYOFF ROUNDS:
AL/NL DIVISION SERIES (Best-of-5)
AL/NL CHAMPIONSHIP SERIES (Best-of-7)
WORLD SERIES (Best-of-7)*

2012
162 GAMES
4 PLAYOFF ROUNDS:
AL/NL WILD CARD SERIES (1 game playoff)
AL/NL DIVISION SERIES (Best-of-5)
AL/NL CHAMPIONSHIP SERIES (Best-of-7)
WORLD SERIES (Best-of-7)*

All of these extra games have pushed the season later and later into the fall. The first World Series ended on October 13, 1903. The 2013 World Series didn't start until October 23. It ended on October 30.

*1903 The first World Series was a best-of-9 format; most since have been best-of-7.

*1904 There was no 1904 World Series. The NL Champions New York Giants refused to play.

*1969 The Championship series were best-of-5 from 1969–1984. They have been best-of-7 since 1985.

The 1981 post-season was a little different. Because of a players' strike mid-season, officials cut the season in two. The best team before the strike played the team with the best record after the strike. The winners advanced to the Championship Series.

*1994 There was no 1994 World Series. A players' strike lasted into the fall, so officials canceled the post-season.

*2012 The winning team today could conceivably play 182+ games to win the World Series. Why the +? Because teams could also end the season tied with another team (or teams) for the last playoff spot. They would also play tie-breaker(s) to determine who gets that last spot.

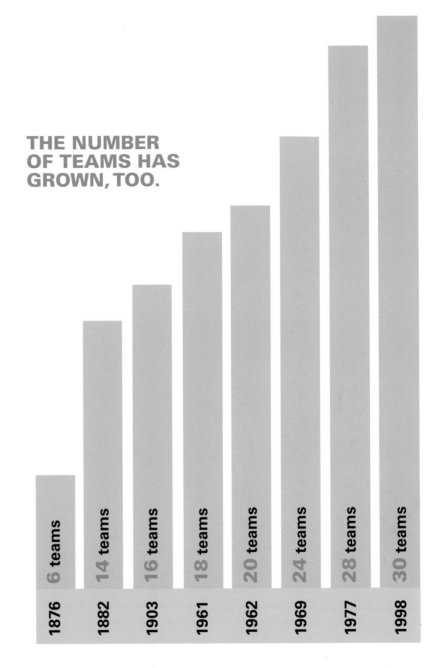

THE NUMBER OF TEAMS HAS GROWN, TOO.

1876	1882	1903	1961	1962	1969	1977	1998
6 teams	14 teams	16 teams	18 teams	20 teams	24 teams	28 teams	30 teams

GRASS VS. TURF

Before 1966, ALL fields were grass. Then Houston built a domed stadium. They tried growing grass, but it all died. So they put a fake field down. It was easy and cheaper to take care of (no mowing, no watering, no fertilizer). By the 1980s, 10 of the 26 major-league fields were carpeted with fake grass.

But many fans and players hated the look, the feel, and the fakeness of turf. In 1992, Baltimore unveiled a new ballpark that looked old—Oriole Park at Camden Yards. It had grass, and it ushered in a new era.

Today there are only two teams with fake turf fields—Toronto and Tampa. Toronto plans to put grass in their stadium in 2015.

BASEBALL TRIVIA

This is the bit in a book where there's usually a list of stuff you should go read, websites you should go visit, et cetera. Unlike baseball, that can be really boring. So instead, what we've got here is some baseball trivia.* Some of the questions are based on things in this book (were you paying attention?) and some are general baseball knowledge.

1. What kinda gross thing was once used as the center of a baseball? (Check back to page 7 if you need a little help.)

2. What is a Texas Leaguer?
a) a minor league player from Dallas
b) a bloop hit that falls in between fielders
c) a five-game winning streak

3. Which team has won the second-most World Series? (Hint: pages 60 and 61 might be worth checking out.)

4. What has happened when a score sheet says there was a 5-3-1 double play? (The numbers 20 and 21 might help you out here.)

5. Tip O'Neill was one of the first superstars in baseball (1883–1892). Where was he born?
a) Australia
b) the United States
c) Canada

6. What is a "walk-off" home run?

7. Which player wore a jersey with #1/8 on the back? (The page with #48 on the bottom is a good place to find this tidbit.)

8. Which of these was not a nickname for Babe Ruth?
a) Iron Horse
b) Bambino
c) Sultan of Swat
d) Jidge

9. What does OPS stand for?

10. List these stadiums in order of highest seating capacity to lowest. To give you some extra info, the capacities are 55,000, 34,000, and 30,000. (You can turn back to page 14 for a little help here.)
a) the Tokyo Dome
b) Oakland-Alameda County Coliseum
c) Dodger Stadium

11. What is Rotisserie Baseball?
a) one of the Korean pre-league divisions
b) a spring training league
c) a fantasy game
d) the name for baseball in France

12. The Baseball Hall of Fame is located in the town where Abner Doubleday—according to legend—organized the first baseball game. The story is a myth, but where did this event reportedly happen?
a) Cooperstown, New York
b) New York City, New York
c) Hackensack, New Jersey
d) Atlanta, Georgia

13. Jackie Robinson was the first African-American player to play in the modern major leagues. (Moses Fleetwood Walker debuted with Toledo in 1884, and there were a handful of African-American players in the very early days of organized baseball.) Robinson's team, the Brooklyn Dodgers, "broke the color barrier" by signing him to a contract. Which MLB team was the last to sign an African-American player?
a) New York Yankees
b) Boston Red Sox
c) Detroit Tigers

14. There are seven ways a hitter can make it to first base. Name them.

15. What award is given to the best defensive player at each position?
a) the Gold Cap
b) the Gold Ball
c) the Gold Cleat
d) the Gold Glove

BONUS QUESTION!
Which player won the most of these golden awards of all time, with 18?
a) Jim Kaat
b) Brooks Robinson
c) Greg Maddux
d) Willie Mays

16. Sandy Koufax, possibly the greatest pitcher of all time, refused to play a game during the 1966 World Series. Why?
a) It was Yom Kippur.
b) He was angry with his manager.
c) He was injured.

17. Korea is baseball crazy. Chan Ho Park was the first South Korean–born player to play in the majors, with the L.A. Dodgers. When did he make his debut?
a) 1974
b) 1984
c) 1994
d) 2004

18. The All-American Girls Professional Baseball League gained many fans during its short life (1943–1954). The Rockford team won a number of league titles (1945, 1948, 1949, and 1950). What was the team nickname?
a) Belles
b) Daisies
c) Peaches
d) Chicks

19. Frank Robinson was the first African-American manager in major league baseball, with Cleveland. What year did he manage his first MLB game?
a) 1955
b) 1965
c) 1975
d) 1985

* The answers and suggestions for "further reading" and websites are listed on pages 68 and 69, but the main point is to have some fun.

THE ANSWERS

1. Fish eyes. They are spongy and rubbery, and were sometimes used in a pinch when rubber and cork weren't available. The Smithsonian Institute has a great website on the history of the baseball. Check it out at: www.smithsonianmag.com/arts-culture/a-brief-history-of-the-baseball-3685086/?no-ist

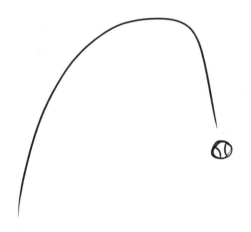

2. A Texas Leaguer is a bloop hit (in other words, not hit well) that falls in between the fielders. No one is quite certain why this is called a Texas Leaguer.

3. The St. Louis Cardinals have won 11 World Series. The New York Yankees lead, by a lot, with 27.

4. The third baseman threw to the first baseman for the first out. The first baseman then threw to the pitcher for the second out.

5. Canada. He wasn't the first Canadian to play. Bill Phillips debuted with the Cleveland Blues in 1879. Both are members of the Canadian Baseball Hall of Fame. baseballhalloffame.ca

6. A "walk-off" home run is one that scores the winning runs in the game. The game ends as soon as the winning run crosses the plate, and everyone walks off the field and goes home.

7. Eddie Gaedel is famous as the shortest player to appear in a major league game. He was 3 feet 7 inches tall (just over one meter) and played one at bat for the St. Louis Browns in 1951. He got a walk.

8. The Iron Horse was actually the nickname for Ruth's teammate, Lou Gehrig. Check out www.baberuth.com for more info on perhaps the greatest ball player of all time.

9. On-base Plus Slugging percentage.

10. Dodger Stadium seats 56,000-plus. The Tokyo Dome seats 55,000-plus. Oakland seats about 34,000. For more on Japanese baseball, check out the book *You Gotta Have Wa* by Robert Whiting. You can also learn more about the Nippon Baseball League at www.npb.or.jp/eng. There are links to more leagues at web.worldbaseballclassic.com and through the International Baseball Federation at www.ibaf.org/en/.

11. Rotisserie Baseball is a kind of fantasy baseball game. Owners get a virtual budget (for example, of $260) and spend it on 20-plus players. Then they get points for leading in certain hitting and pitching categories. It's named for La Rotisserie Française Restaurant in New York City where Daniel Okrent thought up the game while eating with friends.

12. Cooperstown, New York. Why? The story is that Abner Doubleday created the game of baseball in a farmer's field in the town in 1839. The story is nice, but probably not true. Baseball wasn't created in this way, but grew out of similar English games such as cricket and rounders. Doubleday was a famous Civil War general, so perhaps the story was circulated to give the sport a truly American origin story. The Hall of Fame is great to visit, and it also has an amazing website. baseballhall.org.

13. The Boston Red Sox was the last, signing Pumpsie Green in 1959, 12 years after Robinson joined Brooklyn. Cleveland (with Larry Doby) and the St. Louis Browns (with Hank Thompson) also fielded African-American

players in 1947, four months after Robinson's debut. Two years later, Thompson was also the first African-American player for the New York Giants.

14.
1. hit
2. walk
3. hit by pitch
4. error
5. fielder's choice (when the fielders throw another runner out, but let the batter get to first)
6. catcher interference
7. a passed ball on a swinging third strike

15. The Gold Glove.
BONUS answer. Greg Maddux, Hall of Fame pitcher, won an incredible 18 Gold Glove awards. Kaat, also a pitcher, won 16. Brooks Robinson, Baltimore's amazing third baseman, also won 16 in consecutive seasons, from 1960–1975. Willie Mays is famous for making amazing catches with the New York Giants; he won 12 Gold Gloves.

16. The game fell on Yom Kippur, the holiest day on the Jewish calendar. Other Jewish ballplayers have made similar decisions, including the great Hank Greenberg in 1934.

17. 1994. Chan Ho Park was a good pitcher, and played 16 years in the majors. For more on Korean baseball, check out www.koreanbaseball.com (you'll need to translate the page—unless you speak Korean).

18. The Peaches was the nickname for the Rockford team. The others were team names—the Racine Belles, the Fort Wayne Daisies, and the Grand Rapids Chicks. In its 12-year life, the All-American Girls Professional Baseball League (AAGPBL) grew from four teams in 1943 to a high of eight teams in 1946. More than 600 women played in the league. The AAGPBL was almost forgotten, but the movie *A League of Their Own* helped resurrect the history. There's a great website that has all the records and some great photos: www.aagpbl.org.

19. 1975! Although Jackie Robinson and the Dodgers broke the "color barrier" in 1947 and more African-American players were signed by the MLB soon after, it took many years for integration to extend to other roles in the MLB—such as manager, general manager, and owner. The Negro Leagues Baseball Museum is a great place to find out more about the leagues, teams, and players. It's in Kansas City and the website is www.nlbm.com.
Major league baseball also has a site about the Negro Leagues: mlb.mlb.com/mlb/history/mlb_negro_leagues.jsp.

INDEX

McGwire, Mark, 43, 44
McLain, Denny, 32
Mendoza, Mario, 39
Mendoza Line, 39
Meusel, Bob, 42
Milwaukee Brewers, 59
Minnesota Twins, 59
minor leagues, 30, 58
Minoso, Minnie, 49
Mitchell, Jackie, 26
Montgomery, Bob, 11
Montreal Expos, 59
Morales, Kendry, 52

N

Negro Leagues, 15, 49, 69
New York Giants, 51, 65
New York Yankees, 15, 19, 46, 47,
    51, 60, 68
night games, 15
Nippon Baseball League, 68
number system, 20–21
Nuxhall, Joe, 49

O

Oakland A's, 15, 51, 58, 59, 60, 63
Odom, Blue Moon, 21
Oh, Sadaharu, 45
Okrent, Daniel, 68
Olivares, Omar, 21
Olympics, 25
O'Neill, Tip, 22, 66
Oriole Park, 65

P

Paige, Satchel, 49
Park, Chan Ho, 67, 69
Philadelphia Athletics, 59
Phillips, Bill, 68
Pipp, Wally, 31
pitching, 32–33, 34–35, 36, 37, 47
Porray, Ed, 22
Price, David, 36

Q

Quinn, Joe, 22

R

Ramirez, Manny, 53
Rauch, Jon, 48
records, 42–47, 50–51, 57
reliever, 36
revenues, 18
Reynolds, Mark, 39
Robinson, Brooks, 69
Robinson, Frank, 67
Robinson, Jackie, 21, 23, 43, 67, 69
Rodriguez, Alex, 53, 55
Rose, Pete, 45, 50, 53
Roth, Braggo, 42
Rotisserie Baseball, 66, 68
Ruth, Babe, 10, 21, 26, 41, 42–43,
    44, 48, 54, 66, 68
Ryan, Nolan, 31, 49, 51, 55

S

salaries, 17, 19, 54–55
Sánchez, Alex, 53
San Francisco Giants, 61
Schmidt, Mike, 54, 55
Schott, Marge, 27
Scully, Vince, 57
Sisler, George, 42, 51
snacks, cost of, 16–17
Society for American Baseball
    Research, 62
softball, 26
Sosa, Sammy, 44
Spalding, Alexander, 54
Sparks, Steve, 52
stadiums, 14–15, 18, 65, 66, 68
Stargell, Willie, 40
statistics, 32–33, 38–39, 62–63
St. Louis Browns, 45, 59, 68, 69
St. Louis Cardinals, 60, 68
suspensions, 53
Suzuki, Ichiro, 51

T

Texas Leaguer, 66, 68
Texas Rangers, 59, 61
Thompson, Hank, 69
Toledo Mud Hens, 57
travel by teams, 58–59

U

umpires, 11, 49

V

Vander Meer, Johnny, 50
Verlander, Justin, 33
vital statistics, players, 22–23, 48,
    49

W

Wagner, Honus, 38
Waldman, Susyn, 27
Ward, Frank "Piggy," 49
Washington Nationals, 59
Washington Senators, 59
Weaver, Buck, 53
Weber, Jim, 57
West, Joe, 49
Whiting, Robert, 68
Williams, Ted, 39
Wilson, Horace, 24
women, in baseball, 26–27, 67, 69
World Baseball Classic, 23
World Series, 27, 51, 53, 56, 58, 60,
    61, 64, 65, 66, 67, 68

Y

Yankee Stadium, 15
Yastrzemski, Carl, 37
Young, Cy, 32
Young, Walter, 48
Youngblood, Joel, 59
Yount, Robin, 55

Z

Zumaya, Joel, 52

ABOUT KEVIN SYLVESTER

Kevin Sylvester was a horrible baseball player.

He was once knocked out at first base while misplaying a throw from his shortstop.

He threw out his back trying to pitch like Tom Seaver (look him up), and once smacked himself in the face with a Johnny Bench (look him up) Batter-Up kit. You get the idea …

But, he is a lifelong baseball lover. He loves the stats, the improbable plays, and the chance that *anything* can happen at any time. He often describes baseball as the perfect sport for combining brain and body. You can be a physical specimen, but if your head is full of bricks, you'll make too many mistakes to be a good ball player.

Kevin learned about math from the back of baseball cards. Try it sometime. He is a member of SABR (Society for American Baseball Research); he highly recommends that you check them out!

Baseballogy is his latest book with Annick Press. He's also published the financial literacy book *Follow Your Money* (with Michael Hlinka) and behind-the-scenes looks at sports (*Game Day*) and entertainment (*Showtime*).

He's also the author and illustrator of the Neil Flambé Capers, the hockey/Cinderella picture book *Splinters,* and the sports trivia books *Sports Hall of Weird* and *Gold Medal for Weird.* You can find out more about Kevin at kevinsylvesterbooks.com.

Author photo by: Laura Carlin